The Fine Art of Salad Gardening

by E. Annie Proulx

 Rodale Press, Emmaus, Pennsylvania

Printed in the United States of America on recycled paper containing a high percentage of de-inked fiber.

Book design by Anita Noble
Art direction by Karen A. Schell
Interior illustrations by Jean E. Seibert
Recipe testing in the Rodale Test Kitchen: Anita Hirsch, Supervisor of Publication Testing; JoAnn Coponi, Home Economist

Chapters I, II, and IV originally appeared, in shorter and different form, in *Horticulture*.

Library of Congress Cataloging in Publication Data
Proulx, Annie.
    The fine art of salad gardening.

    Bibliography: p.
    Includes index.
    1. Vegetable gardening.   I. Title.
II. Title: Salad gardening.
SB321.P72   1985   635   84-18348
ISBN 0-87857-527-8 hardcover
ISBN 0-87857-528-6 paperback

2 4 6 8 10 9 7 5 3 1 hardcover
2 4 6 8 10 9 7 5 3 1 paperback

For my father, who taught me the delights of the salad bowl

Contents

Introduction

S alads and gardeners have always belonged together, but never more than now, when a keen interest in skillfully prepared, nutritionally balanced food blends with our growing fascination with home gardening. It is an ideal combination, for the cook is able to cut and gather delectable fresh salad materials and rush them at once to the kitchen, there to enjoy the rich store of vitamins, the crisp or silky textures, and the unique flavors at their delicious best. The gardener, thinking of the salads to come, kneels with watering mouth when setting out seedlings.

Salads made from such extraordinarily fresh beginnings are superb, even with simple dressings, but their range and scope are much greater than most American gardeners dream. The gardener who plants a row of iceberg lettuce and some tomatoes and cucumbers under the impression that these are all that's needed for good salads is like a painter restricted to a palette of black and white. There are hundreds of salad greens, each leaf with its own virtue and flavor: some are subtle, some strongly aromatic, some bitter, some juicy and mild, and some so crisp they seem to shatter between the teeth, while others are smooth and liquid, melting on the tongue.

In European markets the salad fancier can choose from dozens of succulent salad greens, kinds that are either unknown in North America or flown in and sold to the carriage trade at outrageous prices—bunches of crisp brooklime; buttery hard cones of Witloof chicons; the spectacular crimson and variegated Italian chicories; the tiny, spicy leaves of rocket just past the seedling stage; creamy, frizzled heads of blanched endives; many local cultivars of tender *mâche;* handfuls of French golden-leaved purslane; the piquancy of salad burnet; half a dozen cresses, from the bitter hoary cress of the eastern Mediterranean to the peppery watercress of the English chalkstreams; lettuces of a hundred sorts, from the cutting types of loose leaf, to sturdy loaves of cos, to melting butterheads. The pale, tasteless iceberg lettuce that dominates American salad bowls is not considered worth growing by many advanced salad lovers.

It is possible to buy some of the more unusual salad greens in urban luxury markets, but these have usually been out of the garden for days, and the prices demanded are staggering. Those of us who want extraordinary and spectacular salads must grow them ourselves. This is one of the most rewarding horticultural specialties a gardener can take up. Beginning growers can develop their skills with some of the salad plants that are easier to grow, and old hands can take on the challenges of the special techniques needed to grow some of the more demanding salad plants to perfection. Searching through seed catalogs for desired cultivars and strains is an absorbing hobby that takes the gardener to some of the small but outstanding specialty seed houses that deal in rarities and exotica, or just the unusual. One can learn much growing a broad range of salad greens, particularly from nineteenth century gardening books and papers, for then, even middle class families employed gardeners who practiced such sophisticated gardening techniques as blanching, forcing, pit-and-frame growing, wintering over, and controlling light and temperature in a dozen ways, all to bring saladings to their finest form. John Evelyn recognized that the skill of the gardener was essential to the fine salad, and he wrote in 1699 in his salad essay, *Acetaria,* "Sallets in general consist of certain *Esculent* Plants and Herbs, improv'd by Culture, Industry, and Art of the *Gard'ner.*"

It is disturbing to those who love the best and simplest foods that the fine salad garden, that tidy bed outside the kitchen door where small and large salads were grown in viridian tints from the pale sea foam of blanched endive to the dark green tongues of *mâche,* seems to have fallen on hard times in this country, replaced by a few dominating bland lettuce cultivars whose character must be "tender" and "sweet" to suit the popular taste. We are losing not only our appreciation for the spicy, savory, bitter and crisp leaves that make truly great salads, but the knowledge of how to grow them. Gardening can be much more than simply strewing seeds in a row and letting nature take its course with a little help from the hoe. Gardeners who have weathered a few seasons might like to try a few of the more advanced techniques that give us the gourmet salad specialties—forcing chicons and Barbe de Capucin, bringing Catalogna chicories of the asparagus type through the winter for an unusual spring harvest of tender little sprouts, trying the winter lettuces, working out planting schedules for continuous supplies of salad leaves, growing the cut-and-come-again types, or bed sowing dozens of kinds of saladings for an early and wonderfully varied salad the Italians call *saladini*, midsummer cluster sowing for autumn lettuce harvests, and a handful of other tricks we can learn from estate and market gardeners of the golden age of salad growing at the turn of the century, as well as from modern experiments.

A salad garden can contain as many as 40 or 50 different plants with flavors from buttery to bitter and textures from melting to crisp. In Europe, the gardener is imaginative in the kitchen and takes pains to grow green salads to perfection. Not just two or three sorts of lettuce, but an extraordinary range of plants, including purslane; *mâche;* salad burnet; a number of cresses; many chicories, from the asparaguslike *puntarelles* to the torpedo-shaped little Witloofs, to the spectacular red Italian regional chicories; curly endive and broad-leaved Batavian endives, each in several specialized strains; rocket and sorrel; field salad; sea kale; chrysanthemums; more than a hundred lettuces, and many, many flowers and herbs. With such rich choices to be harvested from earliest spring to late fall, a gardener can treat a salad as a work of art, constructing fine compositions with an eye for flavor, texture, color, rarity of material, and unusual and piquant taste experiences.

Nor does it stop there. In many parts of the world it is traditional to gather wild plants to add to the domestic salad bowl. Some of our locally famous salad greens such as the Appalachian saxifrage *(Saxifraga micranthidifolia),* or the miner's lettuce *(Montia perfoliata)* of the Pacific coast have a following, but hundreds are neglected. In New England, an excellent salad green is the dark, narrow leaf of the red-seeded dandelion *(Taraxacum erythrospermum),* a smaller, more finely cut plant than the big green common dandelion; this little plant adds a nutty, faintly bitter savor to salads. I pick it 6 feet beyond my garden fence from earliest spring well into summer and rejoice that it's there.

Putting together a gourmet salad garden is an absorbing horticultural hobby that can last your entire life. It will reward you not only with the beauty of plants grown to prefection but with delectable flavors at the table as well. To grow the more sophisticated or unfamiliar salad greens means a search through the offerings of small, specialty seed houses as well as the major seed suppliers. It is worthwhile to write away for the catalogs of European seed houses to get certain cultivars or strains, or even hard-to-find species such as sea kale and garden purslane. Tracking down the seeds of hoary cress or the rosy *radicchio di Treviso* has its own excitement for the salad gardener who longs to try these things.

Your pleasure in a variable salad garden need not be selfish. If you are a small-scale market gardener, you might find it profitable to offer your customers a mixture of 15 to 25 different salad greens picked fresh, washed and packaged as a specialty item, as do some European growers. As the season advances, the character of the mix changes. Over an entire season you might use as many as 50 or 60 different cultivars in these little salad conglomerations. Le Jardin du Gourmet, importers of French garden seed, offers a packet mix of 11 different salad greens in its *Mesclun* sample. It's an easy way to start making the best salads you've ever eaten.

The Fine Art of Salad Gardening makes creating these wonderful salads a snap because it tells you how to grow and harvest dozens of salad plants. Recipes developed especially to use these plants make the task of creating glorious salads effortless. The tasty results range from tart and tangy to smooth and creamy. In addition to these practical matters you'll also learn about the history, folklore, and magic of salad plants, too.

Oh, Green and Glorious!

Sydney Smith, essayist, celebrated wit, gourmet, critic, and clergyman, was a member of a circle of brilliant talkers and writers in the early nineteenth century. One of the Reverend Smith's most intense interests was salads. He cut a swath through the dining rooms of society's great houses correcting the follies committed over salads. Somewhere along the way he wrote a recipe for a "winter salad" dressing in verse. These few lines became so popular they are what Smith is best remembered for, and the demand in his own lifetime for copies, grew until he had bundles of copies specially printed to meet the demand. Although extraordinarily salty to our taste, this recipe deserves to see the light of day again.

To make this condiment your poet begs
The pounded yellow of two hard-boiled eggs;
Two boiled potatoes, passed through kitchen sieve,
Smoothness and softness to the salad give.
Let onion atom lurk within the bowl,
And, half-suspected, animate the whole.
Of mordant mustard add a single spoon,
Distrust the condiment that bites so soon;
But deem it not, thou man of herbs, a fault
To add a double quantity of salt;
Four times the spoon with oil of Lucca crown,
And twice with vinegar procured from town;
And lastly o'er the flavoured compound toss
A magic soupçon of anchovy sauce.
Oh, green and glorious! Oh, herbaceous treat!
'Twould tempt the dying anchorite to eat;
Back to the world he'd turn his fleeting soul,
And plunge his fingers in the salad bowl!
Serenely full, the epicure would say,
'Fate cannot harm me, I have dined today.'

I

The
Epicurean
Lettuces

*W*hat lettuces there are! Frilled edges, curly leaves, speckled and freckled, ruffled and folded, shaped like oak leaves and deers' tongues, growing in tall cones or low rosettes, and in colors from lime green, deep viridian and bronze to ruby, creamy yellow, or variegated combinations such as a delicate green leaf with a dark red border; lettuces with textures that range from a crunchy, crisp snap to a tender, melting smoothness; flavors from the tasty, savory cos to the delicate, buttery Bibbs.

Ancient Lettuce

The beautiful lettuce is a member of the Composite family. Lettuce is a domesticated plant whose various cultivars come in many shapes and colors. The ancestor of these beauties is *Lactuca serriola,* a biennial that grew wild in Asia, Eurasia, and the Mediterranean countries in the remote prehistoric past. But from the beginnings of civilization people have cultivated lettuce, and it has been the queen of the salad bowl for millennia, appreciated by the Sumerians, Egyptians, Greeks, and Romans. There was more to lettuce than just its table qualities. An Egyptian fertility god, Min, was showered with offerings of lettuce, for both the Assyrians and the Egyptians thought the milky lettuce juice had aphrodisiacal qualities.

In those far-past centuries lettuce did not head up but grew its large leaves on a thick, tall stalk. It probably looked very much like modern lettuce when it bolts and thrusts its thick central stalk up to the sky, or like the oriental stem lettuces rarely grown in this country. It was the stalk, in fact, which identified some early cultivars. The Greek philosopher Theophrastus wrote of four distinct lettuce types—the FLAT-STALKED, the ROUND-STALKED, the LACONIA and the sweet, tender WHITE lettuce. This last was also known as "poppy lettuce" for its soporific qualities. Lettuce was an important part of the Greek diet and is mentioned by Galen, Aristotle, and Hippocrates.

But it was those ardent and excellent gardeners, the ancient Romans, who brought lettuce to a head through generations of careful selection and seed saving. The beautiful lettuces were esteemed in late Rome by gourmet voluptuaries who propped themselves on their elbows and feasted endlessly on every delicacy that could be imagined, from ostrich brains and roasted thrushes

2

to dormice dipped in honey and rolled in poppyseed. Lettuce, said Pliny, was cooling and pleasant to eat in the summer, good for the digestion, and it gave one an appetite. He listed no less than nine cultivars grown for the Roman salad: ALBA, CAECILIAN, CAPPADOCIAN, CRISPA, GRAECA, LACONICON, NIGRA, PURPUREA, and RUBENS. It is amusing to speculate about the appearance and characters of these early salad lettuces. The Alba is probably the same as the Greek White lettuce, and Pliny said that in early times this was the only lettuce known in Italy. Laconica or Laconia were names for Sparta, where we can guess the Laconicon cultivar was developed. Cappadocian lettuce perhaps came from the region Cappadocia in Asia Minor, now eastern Turkey. Graeca means simply "the Greek lettuce," and Caecilian lettuce may have been a type developed by the Roman family clan named Caecilius. Crispa refers to crinkly, curly leaves, while Purpurea (purple) and Rubens (red) tell us the Romans enjoyed these handsome red-tinged lettuces. Niger means the color black, but this may have referred to the color of the lettuce seed rather than a dark leaf—perhaps a kind of early BLACK-SEEDED SIMPSON.

Columella, an agricultural writer of sorts who lived in the first century A.D., gives us a recipe for preserving lettuce that sounds like an early version of sauerkraut. The leaves were stripped off the stalks and soaked in brine, then the excess salt was rinsed away, and the leaves were packed in a vinegar-brine mixture. Tacitus ate bowls of lettuce before retiring for the night, counting on the soporific qualities of lettuce to put him to sleep, and Caesar Augustus fancied himself cured of an illness by the powers of lettuce and erected a statue to the noble plant.

This reputation of lettuce as a tranquilizer is very ancient, and in the early pharmacopoeia it was regarded as a mild kind of opium without the deleterious effects of that narcotic. There are references in medieval literature to lettuce juice dried into brown wafers that were used to induce a narcotic sleep in insomniacs, the painfully ill or wounded, and people going under the surgeon's knife. The process of making these lettuce wafers is decribed in the following excerpt from William Rhind's *A History of the Vegetable Kingdom*, published in Glasgow in 1855:

As soon as the flower stems have attained a considerable size and height, but before the flowers begin to expand, a portion of the top is cut off transversely. This operation is performed when the sun has excited the plants into powerful action. The

Growing Techniques from the Past

The growing techniques of gardeners in ages past to get the plumpest, most frilly and sweetest lettuces were at once sophisticated and naively credulous. Giovanni Baptista Porta, in his late sixteenth century book *Natural Magick,* a best-seller not only in its day but for centuries afterwards, tells readers how to grow enormous lettuces, how to blanch them, how to give them fragrances and make them sweet. His procedures may strike modern gardeners as somewhat innocent:

Make Great Lettice

You must remove them, and water them well; and when they are grown half a handful high, you must dig round about them, that the roots may be seen; then wrap them in Ox-dung, and cover them over again, and water them still; and when they are waxen bigger, cut the leaves cross with a sharp knife, and lay upon them a little barrel or tub that never was pitched, (for Pitch will hurt the herb) that so it may grow not in height, but onely spread forth in breadth.

Blanched salad greens were esteemed greatly in earlier days before it was recognized how rich in vitamins the dark leaves were. Sometimes blanching was practiced to soften the bitterness of the sharper salad plants, such as endive and chicory. Here Porta tells us how to "whiten" lettuce:

milky juice quickly exudes from the wound, while the heat of the sun renders it immediately so viscid, that it does not flow down in a liquid state, but concretes around the part whence it issues, forming a brownish scale, about the size of a sixpence. When it has acquired the proper consistence it is removed, and as the inspissated juice closes up the extremities of the divided vessels, it is necessary to cut off another small piece of the stem; this causes the escape of the juice again, and another scale is formed. The same process is repeated as long

A Lettice may be made white,
as Florentinus sheweth. If you would, saith he, procure goodly white Lettice, then must you bind together the tops of the leaves, two dayes before they be gathered; for so they will be fair and white. Likewise you may whiten them by casting sand upon them.

It was something of a showman gardener's trick then to impart unusual fragrances to fruits and vegetables, and Porta shows how to make lemons smell like cinnamon, artichokes with the scent of roses, and flowers redolent of cloves. Lettuce was no exception, though gardeners who followed Porta's advice on this one probably only tried it once.

He writes:

So we have procured Odoriferous Lettice,
by taking the seed of Lettice, and putting it into the seed of a Citron, and so planting it.

And for gardeners who long for a sweet lettuce, here is a favorite medieval way of sympathetic gardening:

Sweet Lettice
for if you water them in the evening with new sweet wine, and let them drink for three evenings together as much of that liquor as they will soak up, it will cause sweet Lettice, as *Aristoxenus* the Cyrenian hath taught out of *Athenæus*.

as the weather is favorable, or the plant will yield any juice.

The sleep-inducing power of the plant is related to the presence in the latex sap of triterpenoid alcohols. In Rhind's day these wafers were made and dispensed under the name *Lactucarium,* and a drug known today as *Lactucarium germanillium* or "lettuce opium" is still produced from the sap of *Lactuca virosa.*

The Romans brought the glories of lettuce to England, as well as the Latin name for it. The botanical *Lactuca sativa* refers to the milky liquid that comes from the stem; *lac* means "milk," and *lactuca* is literally a reference to ". . . the thing having milklike juice. . . ." As lettuce spread through Europe and England, the plant worked its way into local folklore. Oddly enough, its character now was quite the opposite of the lust-provoking aphrodisiac of the old Egyptians; now lettuce was used sometimes in a poultice to calm mens' unruly sexual appetites, and it had the reputation of being a sterile plant. Too much lettuce growing in a garden could have a negative effect on a wife's fertility. Lettuce was also thought to prevent hangovers if it was eaten after the wine was drunk.

A very curious little passage on lettuce and a minuscule devil is quoted in Bridget Ann Henisch's *Fast and Feast: Food in Medieval Society* (1977). She illustrates the danger of failing to say grace before a medieval meal by citing the example of a girl who ate a lettuce leaf before the blessing was said. "Invisible to her, a devil happened to be sitting on the leaf at the time. Once swallowed, he refused to come out again, and the priest who arrived to exorcise him heard through the girl's lips an aggrieved little voice complaining: 'Allas! whatt hafe I done? I satt upon the letes, and sho come and tuke me up and bate me.' "

By 1629, John Parkinson could write in his delightful *Paradisi in Sole, Paradisus Terrestris* that there were so many kinds of lettuce that if he named them all he would scarcely be believed. He describes "cabbage" lettuces, the "Romane or red lettuce . . . the best and greatest of all the rest," a white Roman lettuce that must be bleached, and a Virginia lettuce with ruddy leaves (which he remarks is "not of any regard"). He lists Lumbard lettuce, a loose-leaf type, several curly-leaf lettuces, and a winter lettuce. All of these, he says, are "spent in sallets, with oil and vinegar . . . while they are fresh and greene, or whited. . . . They all cool a hot and fainting stomacke . . . procureth rest and taketh away the paines of the head: bound likewise to the cods, it helpeth . . . restraineth immoderate lust. . . ."

The greatest salad champion of all was John Evelyn, who wrote ecstatically of lettuce in the *Acetaria,* declaring that it "ever was, and still continues the principle Foundation of the universal *Tribe* of Sallets." He describes lettuce as follows:

And certainly 'tis not for nothing that our Garden-Lovers, and *Brothers of the Sallet,* have been so exceedingly industrious to cultivate this Noble Plant, and multiply its Species; for to name a few in present use: we have the *Alphange* of *Montpelier*, crisp and delicate; the *Arabic; Ambervelleres; Belgrade, Cabbage, Capuchin, Cofs-Lettuce, Curl'd;* the *Genoa* (lasting all the Winter) the *Imperial, Lambs,* or *Agnine,* and *Lobbs* or *Lop-Lettuces.* The *French Minion* a dwarf kind: the *Oak-Leaf, Passion, Roman, Shell,* and *Silefian,* hard and crimp (esteemed of the best and rarest) with divers more.

Evelyn's list contains all of the major lettuce groups we know today—head lettuce, loose-leaf lettuce, curly lettuce, cutting lettuces and cos.

American Lettuce

John Winthrop, Jr., the son of the Colonial governor Winthrop, brought packets of vegetable seeds to the New World from England. His famous 1631 "bill of garden seeds" from the London grocer who sold them has survived the centuries, and included among the "hartichockes" and "spynadg" and "cabedg" seed is the note of "3 oz lettice seeds 2d per oz." But the first lettuce planted in North America was sown and picked by Samuel de Champlain and his men on an island in the Saint Croix River in Maine. Lettuces, sorrel, and cabbages were planted in the gardens of a temporary settlement, and Champlain's drawing of the neat, patterned gardens and the row of buildings exists in the 1619 edition of *Les Voyages.* And Captain John Smith, sailing along the Maine coast, took the time to plant a garden on a small island. He wrote in his journal, "I made a garden upon the top of a Rockie Ile in 43.1/2, 4 leagues from the Main in May, that grew so well, as it served us for sallets in June and July." The accounts and letters of the early settlers in the Colonies frequently mention the "sallets" they have grown and enjoyed.

By the eighteenth century, lettuce growing in America had become quite sophisticated. In 1753, the Reverend Edward Holyoke of Salem, Massachusetts, wrote in his diary that he had planted gourds, cucumbers, and lettuces under glass on February 19 in his "hotbed," which should have allowed him to dine on fresh "sallet" in early April, while snowdrifts still lay deep in the woods.

Steadily a taste for lettuce grew, though salads were, for the great mass of people, ignored in favor of pork, cornmeal, bread, potatoes, and beans. Salads were thought to be somewhat effete and sissified until the twentieth century, when nutritional studies demonstrated how vital green leafy vegetables are in the diet. In the early nineteenth century, market and truck gardens outside large cities like Philadelphia, Boston, and New York were growing acres of lettuce under glass. Boston was a particularly important lettuce market, and many commercial lettuce growers forced lettuce through much of the year to supply that city with salad makings. *The New England Farmer* of 1853 shows a "Boston hotbed" kept warm by decomposing horse manure beneath the root zone of the plants. These glass hotbeds were covered over with thick straw mats at night against the chilly temperatures and were protected from wind by fences. A favorite cultivar—TENNIS-BALL—was a diminutive, sweet dwarf head lettuce. It could be served in a small bowl as an individual salad and was much fancied at dinner parties. In 1838, Thorburn's seed catalog offered American growers 13 lettuces, but in 1883, the great seed house and vegetable information source, Vilmorin-Andrieux, named 114 distinct kinds of lettuce in green, bronze, red, spotted and variegated colors, and of every imaginable shape and texture.

Local lettuces developed by backyard, salad-loving gardeners were not uncommon, and the seed of a good local lettuce was preferred to mail-order types by many. Even today some gardeners can remember getting vegetable seed from a neighbor who had especially good strains of homebred plants. The first seed catalog put out by Harris Seeds in 1879 carries a good lettuce story by the company's founder, Joseph Harris, that illustrates the movement of a local lettuce out of the home garden and into the national market in those days when amateur gardeners took pleasure in developing vegetable specialties instead of leaving it all to professional breeders. Wrote Mr. Harris:

Living near me, is an industrious German woman, who some years ago was left a widow with several young children. The relatives of the husband tried to get the small farm away from her, but with the advice and assistance of my friend and neighbor "The Deacon," the widow was enabled to hold the farm, and since then she has been a very successful and prosperous market gardener. She is especially noted for her large, fine lettuce, for which, no matter how overstocked the market may be, she always manages to find customers willing to pay her a good price. She is very careful to save her own seed from the best plants, and has done so for years, till she has now undoubtedly got a very superior lettuce. Out of gratitude to the Deacon, she has from year to year given him a little of the seed, and the Deacon has always beaten me in lettuce. I never quite liked to acknowledge this. I was obliged to admit that he had larger and handsomer heads of lettuce than any to be found in my garden, but then, as to quality, as tastes differ, there was a chance for argument! And so the matter has stood. Finally the widow was kind enough to give me a little of her selected seed also, and I am obliged to admit that I have never raised any lettuce that gave so much satisfaction. On this farm it goes by the name of the "Deacon's Lettuce." I do not know that it has any other name. If it is an old kind, as it may be, it has been undoubtedly greatly "improved" by the careful cultivation and persistent selection of the widow.

Harris goes on then to offer some of the "Deacon's Lettuce" seed to the public. It is hoped that he gave the widow—she is not dignified by her name—a percentage of the returns from the sale of the seed.

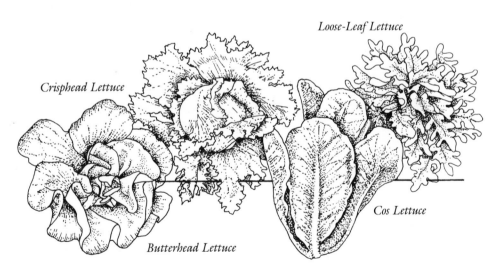

Loose-Leaf Lettuce

Crisphead Lettuce

Cos Lettuce

Butterhead Lettuce

Lettuces Today

Today there are hundreds of lettuce cultivars grown all over the world, some suited to a narrow range of climatic conditions, such as the superb English lettuces that have been developed in the moist, cool, cloudy atmosphere of the British Isles, or the

Chinese stem lettuces, valued for their fleshy, tender stalks rather than the leaves. A gardener with a taste for salads can make an ambitious hobby of seeking out and growing as many different cultivars as he or she can find. It is absorbing and entertaining to test-grow eight or ten different lettuces each year, to rate them on their preformance in the garden and flavor at the table—after all, how they taste is what really matters. At least 100 different lettuce cultivars are offered in North American seed catalogs, and at least one seed house—The Cook's Garden in Londonderry, Vermont—specializes in lettuces. Ambitious gardeners can write for foreign seed catalogs and keep an eye out for seed packets of new kinds of lettuce when they travel. The result is wonderful lettuces of extraordinary flavor, unusual appearance, and interesting habits of growth.

A lettuce statistician reported in the *New York Times* a couple of years ago that Americans eat almost 30 pounds of lettuce per year per capita, and that about three billion heads of commercial lettuce are grown annually for this astonishing market. Lettuce is the fastest-moving item in the supermarket; more heads of lettuce slide past the checkout register than quarts of milk or loaves of bread. It's too bad that most of this salad material is the pale, tasteless iceberg lettuce that some wit has called "California's biggest export—water, in a lettuce-shaped container." These heads have been bred for uniformity, disease resistance, ability to travel long distances without rotting or showing wilt, long shelf life, and ability to make "a nice appearance" in the carton. Flavor and texture are relatively unimportant. By the time these lettuces get to the produce bins they have been stripped of their outer leaves and wrapped in plastic; they closely resemble bowling balls of a greenish-white hue and are utterly lackluster in salads. Yet so ubiquitous are they, that consumers—including many otherwise sensible gardeners—will bypass locally grown leaf or soft-head lettuces in favor of these elderly hard heads, which they take home and proceed to tear into fragments the size of leaf lettuce! Many gardeners ignore the evidence of their taste buds and work hard and unsuccessfully to grow head lettuce while the easier, more flavorful and beautiful loose leafs, butterheads, and cos lettuces are neglected.

Head lettuces are built for handling. The epicurean garden lettuces have been bred for *taste*. They do not travel well and wilt a few hours out of the garden, so they are best grown near the kitchen door and used very shortly after they are gathered.

Some local producers of butterhead and loose-leaf lettuces where I live in Vermont market them with the cut stem wrapped in damp vermiculite in a small plastic bag. The deep green fresh rosettes stay firm and healthy and beautiful for days—yet many shoppers bypass them and choose watery iceberg lettuces of inferior flavor. John Randolph, Jr., of Virginia (1727–1784) in his *Treatise on Gardening,* did not care greatly for the head lettuces either, remarking "this sort of Lettuce is the worst of all the kinds in my opinion. It is the most watery and flashy, does not grow to the size that many of the other sorts will do, and very soon runs to seed."

Home gardeners have the most wonderful opportunity to escape from the tyranny of commercial iceberg lettuce to the delights of dozens and dozens of green-leaf salad delicacies, some bred to grow in the short seasons of the far North or in greenhouses or forcing frames, some in tropical regions or cloudy, damp climates. *Lactuca sativa* is generally divided into four major groups—the crisphead, butterhead, cos, and loose leaf. There are intermediate crosses that don't fall comfortably into any of these categories, such as CRISP AS ICE, a cross between a butterhead and a crisphead, or WALLOP, a cross between a crisphead and a cos type. Increasingly, lettuces developed for seasonal uses are crossing the Atlantic to our gardens, so that the terms "spring lettuce," "summer lettuce," and "winter lettuce" are becoming familiar to American gardeners. From Europe we are starting to experiment with cut-and-come-again lettuces, developed to produce a continuous crop of salad leaves that are harvested repeatedly every ten days or so. Every year the seed catalogs offer a few new lettuces, first-time introductions or imports, and often they are suited to difficult climates. Gardeners should keep an eye open for new introductions in the lettuce sections of seed catalogs each spring. Always try growing a few unfamiliar types, for experimentation makes gardening an entertainment and a pleasurable hobby.

Crisphead Lettuce *(Lactuca sativa* var. *capitata)*

The crisphead lettuces are also called cabbage head and iceberg in the older literature. The leaf rosette has an enlarged bud that forms a tight, dense head, firm and heavy, and often of a pale green to silvery white color. These lettuces are more than 90 percent water, and irrigation of some sort is necessary to grow them properly. They are the commercial heads of the supermarket produce counter, much grown in North America, especially in California and around the Great Lakes. They are not yet very important abroad, though a survey of gardening periodicals from overseas shows both gardeners and consumers have an increasing interest in crispheads. These head lettuces lack flavor, but the crisp and juicy texture is delightful to many people, and one can easily discover the seeds for almost a dozen commercial crispheads in our seed catalogs. The following are a few of the more common crispheads.

ITHACA (72 days to maturity) is a commercial lettuce that was developed at Cornell University by Dr. Peter Minotti. It is a good green color and is fringed on the leaf edges. Like most commercial lettuces, there is great uniformity of type and maturity date, which is generally in midseason. Ithaca is a heavy yielder that is resistant to tipburn and brown rib diseases and grows well both on upland and muck.

ICEBERG is a familiar head lettuce that has been around for years. It is compact, with tight, medium-size heads and few outer leaves. Inside, the firm and very crisp hearts blanch to a silvery yellow color. The plant is vigorous and hardy, but drinks up tremendous amounts of water.

There are several GREAT LAKES lettuce strains, and these dominate agribusiness fields, for they are very uniform in development and appearance, slow to bolt, and hold well in hot weather. EARLY GREAT LAKES (75 days) heads out very dependably, with a firm, solid head, and slightly fringed and ruffled outer leaves. The texture is brittle and juicy. Great Lakes (82 days) is widely planted, even in the South, where it is used as an early winter crop, though the type also does very well in the North and East. It resists cold damage and rarely sunburns or suffers tipburn. The heads are large, glistening, and of a rich green. The leaf edges are fringed and ruffled. Great Lakes will hold well in hot weather, which makes it a good cultivar for late sowing. There are several strains of Great Lakes carried by Stokes Seeds, including GREAT LAKES 6238, PREMIER GREAT LAKES, and the late-season GREAT LAKES 659 that tolerates more cold than the others.

MONTELLO is a recent introduction from the Wisconsin Cooperative Extension Service. It matures in 70 to 75 days and has high tolerance to corky root rot disease. The heads are very large and vigorous and of a rich, dark green color. Montello is very heat tolerant and will head when some of the older Great Lakes cultivars bolt or fail to head up. This lettuce is grown in the North, the South, and the West and is praised by buyers as having a nice appearance in the box. It resists splitting because the heads are a little looser than most crisphead types.

MESA 659 is a big-headed, slow-growing lettuce that is very tolerant to frost. MINETTO, offered by Burpee (80 days), makes small, hard, tight heads and matures about 10 days earlier than most head types. It is resistant to tipburn and is a dependable header. It takes up less space in the home garden than some of the large crisphead types. Park Seed hails MISSION as a new iceberg type that will head up in warm-climate home gardens. It makes tight, pale heads 6 to 8 inches in diameter and has outstanding heat resistance. The long outer leaves are deeply cut and fringed.

PENNLAKE (88 days) is a commercial cross between Great Lakes and IMPERIAL 847, another older head lettuce. MINILAKE (80 days) matures a week earlier than Pennlake and has larger heads than Minetto. This is a dark green lettuce, very uniform, giving high yields, and the earliest of the commercial head lettuces. It has a short center core, and better flavor and quality than most commercially grown lettuces.

There are a handful of New York-type head lettuces around in the catalogs, too. Most were developed at Cornell University and are well suited to northern New York's agricultural belt. Some of these are CORNELL 456, an early, dense-headed lettuce that tipburns fairly easily; Imperial 847, an early, hardheaded plant developed to withstand hot weather; and NEW YORK 12, another heat-resistant lettuce that holds well. The old NEW YORK NONPAREIL dates back before 1906, when these very large, extremely hard heads were quite popular.

Only a few imported crispheads turn up in our catalogs. TÊTE DE GLACE, from Belgium, makes a very crisp, almost crackling large head and has a superior flavor, rich and somewhat nutty. WEBB'S WONDERFUL (64 days) is heat resistant, slow to bolt, and gives large, crisp heads. It is a standard in British vegetable gardens, but growers here may find it does not do so well. Because it is heat resistant and a rapid grower, it has been recommended for gardens in the South. AVONCRISP is very similar to Webb's Wonderful, and in England is often used as a cut-and-come-again crop—the young plants are harvested with a knife before they head up, which allows them to force another crop of crisp leaves. WINDERMERE (66 days) is another English crisphead that grows small but very crisp heads. It is a good summer lettuce that withstands heat and drought, and is slow to bolt. Southern gardeners might want to try it. MARMER makes a hard iceberg head in 75 days, and it is generally a forced greenhouse lettuce sown November through February for the early spring harvest.

It's interesting to note that in *Encyclopedia of Gardening* J. C. Loudon, the famous horticultural authority of the early nineteenth century, remarks that the head lettuces were not often used for salads—the cos lettuces were considered the best salad material—but in soups.

Crisphead lettuces are more demanding to grow than other types. With the older cultivars and many of the imported head lettuces, a burst of summer heat early in the season can send the flower stalk burgeoning up through the center of the immature head. Most home gardeners will want to leave the head lettuces to the commercial growers and concentrate on the choicer types.

Butterhead Lettuce *(Lactuca sativa* var. *capitata)*

Technically butterhead lettuces are in the same taxonomic basket as the crispheads, but the differences in texture and appearance are considerable. Tender, floppy leaves, and buttery, melting hearts are typical of the soft-leaf butterheads. They are so tender they can be bruised while being picked, and they do not travel well at all. BIBB and the several BOSTON lettuces are the best known in this group. Bibb is an expensive, exquisite, subtle specialty lettuce sometimes called Kentucky limestone lettuce. It was developed by an amateur horticulturist in Frankfort, Kentucky, John J. Bibb. One finds it in luxury hotels and restaurants in individual salads, but it is infamous for bolting in hot weather. The outer leaves are loosely folded over the buttery yellow inner heart. SUMMER BIBB is an improved strain developed by the well-known lettuce breeder, Dr. George Raleigh, of Cornell University, and it can stand the heat. BURPEE BIBB is a recent release that has replaced the old FORDHOOK butterhead in the

Burpee catalog. This lettuce, which the catalog says is "far superior to regular Bibb," is slow to bolt and resistant to tipburn. The little heads are well suited to growing in containers or even hanging planters, and city gardeners might like to try growing them in a window box for a very special dinner party. BUTTER-CRUNCH is a Bibb type that takes 65 to 75 days to maturity. It was an All-America Winner and is another of Dr. Raleigh's triumphs. It has greater heat resistance than Bibb and a tighter, heavier head than most butterheads. It is a vigorous grower and holds two weeks longer than Bibb; the leaves stay quite sweet even after the plant goes to seed.

Boston lettuce is a tender, high-quality butterhead. One of the best of the group is DARK GREEN BOSTON (68 to 80 days), which is very popular in restaurants and home gardens. Dark Green Boston has an excellent flavor, rich and full. The texture is smooth and melting. This cultivar has largely eclipsed the older WHITE BOSTON, which was the standard for years. Many improved strains have sprung from the old White Boston. Two commercial greenhouse or hydroponic production lettuces from Europe are Boston types—CAPITAN and OSTINATA. Capitan is very large and early (62 days) and a favorite with the greenhouse growing crowd. Ostinata is smaller but a high-yielding, dependable short-season lettuce that reaches maturity in eight weeks. Both of these are available from Stokes Seeds. HILDE is a GIANT WHITE BOSTON from France (65 to 79 days), where it is popular for both spring and autumn sowing. It is a rapid grower, and it must be grown quickly to be at its best. It is a big, yellow green plant in the garden, and although English gardeners enjoy several Hilde strains not available here, I found Hilde the most uninteresting of the butterhead lettuces.

TOM THUMB is a miniature butterhead that is in vogue just now; it is quite popular in restaurants served up as individual salads just as the little Tennis-Ball was in the great Victorian restaurants. The tender, crumpled leaves unfold around a petite heart. Although some seedsmen describe it as a "new" lettuce, Shepherd Ogden, Vermont lettuce grower and scholar, points out the entry for Tom Thumb lettuce in the 1885 English edition of *The Vegetable Garden* of the famous French seed company, Vilmorin-Andrieux et Cie.

European butterheads are generally considered the finest of all. Every year a few more of them are listed in our specialty seed house catalogs as the word gets around among gardeners. ALL

THE YEAR ROUND turned up in a 1983 Epicure catalog, described as an English black-seeded midseason lettuce that can stand hot, dry weather and is slow to bolt. A pale green leaf with a melting but crisp texture made it sound very inviting, and it was recommended to southern gardeners. Three plantings of it failed in my garden during an unusually hot and dry summer. Other gardeners may have better success. Thompson and Morgan say All the Year Round can be sown at any time, but William Dam cautions that it is for "early sowings." (Lettuce seed does not germinate well in soil temperatures above 68°F.)

COBHAM GREEN (62 days) is another English butterhead, which is heat resistant and has a handsome dark green color and petite size that makes it useful in interplantings. MERVEILLE DES QUATRES SAISONS from France is a beautiful lettuce, very popular in French restaurants and prized by salad gardeners. This one should be tried by every salad lover. It is crisp and tender at once, slow to bolt, and the clear green leaves are edged dramatically with cranberry red. Lettuce authority Shepherd Ogden grows 30 to 50 fine lettuce cultivars each season for restaurants and the salad trade. Merveille des Quatres Saisons is one of his favorites. He writes:

> Four Seasons wins the color contest hands down. It is not just beautiful, though. I have been able to get good stands from first planting to last, and have had very little trouble with bolting. I think the position of red lettuce—which has constantly been selected against in most breeding programs—is like that of black sheep. When the Standard of Perfection was the only standard around, they were both jettisoned in the name of uniformity and productivity. Now that these qualities have taken on the feeling of a Tooker painting, we are seeing a resurgence of these more colorful breeds and varieties, as well as the return of heirloom varieties.

Two similar lettuces (these are planted in mid-August and wintered over in mild climates for an early spring harvest) are REINE DE MAI and MAI KÖNIG—MAY QUEEN and MAY KING. May King was originated by an unknown gardener in Saxony in the late nineteenth century and still remains one of the best European wintered-over lettuces. It is almost impossible to find in our seed catalogs, for wintering over lettuces is an unfamiliar technique to most North American gardeners. May-Queen is available from

William Dam and sometimes Epicure. This Belgian lettuce (60 days) has clear green leaves tipped with red, small heads and is one of the earliest butterheads. It can be wintered over or sown very early in cold frames or winter greenhouses.

PATIENCE, also from Belgium, is a midseason lettuce of very fine flavor and is fairly resistant to heat; it is at its best grown early in the season. The germination rates are poor if the seed is sown in midsummer for a fall crop.

PIRAT is the German "Sprenkel" lettuce—"speckled lettuce" in translation—a crisp, creamy heart with light green leaves freckled and dotted with a warm, brownish bronze. The flavor is unique, and most lettuce fanciers give it very high marks. Epicure sometimes carries the seed.

KAGRANER SOMMER is another German lettuce, one of the best European butterheads around, a favorite in Europe for decades. It makes good yields, is slow to bolt, and withstands the summer heat very well. Its dependability and fast-maturing habit make it a garden standard abroad for most salad gardeners. In recent years, several new strains of Kagraner have appeared that are even more enticing. ZOMERKONIG (64 days) from Holland is one of these improved Kagraner strains; it is virus resistant, more resistant to bolt than its ancestor, and takes dry, hot midsummer weather quite well. This is a butterhead southern gardeners might find a good bet to grow. ORFEO is another improved Kagraner that matures in only 58 days, tolerates heat well like the others, and produces large, tender, yellow green heads.

TANIA is an outstanding English butterhead available only through Harris Seeds. It is a vivid green color and is mildew resistant (important in the English climate), and, although it cannot take hot midsummer weather, it has excellent flavor and is a good one to grow in the early spring salad garden, or where the climate is cool and cloudy, such as the Canadian Maritimes, the Pacific Northwest, and perhaps high altitude gardens.

Two other butterhead types worth trying are AUGUSTA and BUTTER KING. Augusta (68 days) is a very sweet lettuce with a silky, melting texture. It makes large, medium green heads and has thick, heavy leaves. Augusta is tolerant of heat and resistant to disease. Butter King was developed in Canada and is an improved butterhead twice as large as most Boston types but otherwise similar. It is quite heat tolerant.

BRONZE MIGNONETTE has been around for a while. It is a quick-maturing lettuce (50 days) with outer leaves of bronze-tinted green around a small cream-colored heart. GREEN MIGNONETTE (65 days) is a crisp, sweet lettuce that is small and compact but favored for warm climate salad gardens. Nichols Garden Nursery's Catalog says that it is often grown in tropical countries. Southern gardeners might like to put it to the test.

Most of the European butterheads are available from Le Jardin du Gourmet, Epicure, Thompson and Morgan, and William Dam, though Epicure has reduced its seed offerings since the sale of the company to Herbst Seeds in 1982. Salad growers will be rewarded by annually studying the catalogs of these companies, which often add new (to us) imported lettuces, chicories, small salads, and endive in oustanding strains well suited to the private garden. The J. L. Hudson catalog can also be very rewarding for salad growers.

There are some problems with growing butterheads. Both butterheads and loose-leaf lettuces have soft, tender leaves, and in heavy rain, high winds or hail, they can be severely bruised and even ruined. A sheltered place with perhaps a shade cover goes a long way toward protecting these tender dainties. Almost all of the lettuces benefit from being grown under a light shade cloth (available from garden supply stores and mail-order houses).

Cos Lettuce *(Lactuca sativa* var. *longifolia)*

Cos is also called romaine lettuce. It has both these names because the Romans (great lettuce fanciers who were always on the watch for good salad material) discovered it on the Greek island of Cos where it still grows abundantly. It was brought back to Rome and became so widely grown there that later travelers identified it with the city. When the papacy removed to Avignon in the period of the so-called Babylonian Captivity, cos lettuce came with them to be grown in the papal gardens and became known in France as romaine lettuce. Most of the cos types are remarkably resistant to heat and strong sunlight, both outstanding climatic influences on the island of Cos.

Cos lettuces are tall and cylindrical, with long, green oval leaves and a crisp, paler green heart. The midribs are thick and juicy. Cos lettuce stands up better under salad bowl tossing than the butterheads and is far more flavorful than the crispheads. This leaf strength, as well as the rich flavors, make it an indispensable ingredient in Caesar salads, one of the great culinary inventions of our time—reputedly first made in a restaurant in Mexico City during the 1920s, and gradually moving north until it became a California favorite. Cos can even hold its own against the pungency of a blue cheese dressing.

In England, gardeners often tie a bit of raffia around the middle of the cos lettuce when it is about three-quarters grown; this helps it form a blanched inner head, nutty in flavor, the color of buttery Jersey cream, and crisp and tender.

PARIS WHITE COS is one of those old cultivars that has been around for generations and is still a leading plant. It is prized for its mild, sweet flavor, and was listed in the first Harris Seeds catalog as "best and most popular of the Cos lettuce." Many seed houses still offer it. The heads are tightly folded, the inner leaves a rich yellow cream color with crunchy midribs, and the taste crisp and subtle. Paris White grows about 10 inches tall, and because the leaves fold over the top, it does not need tying to urge head development. It takes about 83 days to mature and is slow to bolt. It plays an excellent role as a more delicate leaf when continuous sowings are made and the leaves harvested while the plant is immature—this makes a very fine and subtle salad. PARRIS ISLAND COS is a fast grower (76 days) with excellent vigor and probably the most popular romaine with the seed catalog people. It is widely grown commercially, and this is probably the romaine you get at the produce counter. It is a very uniform plant, somewhat tolerant of lettuce mosaic, and it grows well in cooler climates. I personally find Parris Island one of the more inferior cos types—coarser in texture and less flavorsome than others. Both Paris White and Parris Island seeds are easy to find, while the old French market cultivar ROMAINE BLONDE MARAÎCHÈRE, with its big long head and distinctive pale green color, has turned up only in Le Jardin du Gourmet and Epicure catalogs, to my knowledge. This is an old cos, but a very good one, once grown both for early spring markets as well as through the summer. Early spring crops of this cos must be protected by glass cloches or cold frames, since this type is more sensitive to frost than most. Turn-of-the-century French gardening books mention bronze-leaf cos lettuces cultivated in the Midi, and older references mention the SPOTTED COS, apparently a speckled type now lost to gardeners.

The VALMAINE is a savoyed cos with thick leaves that grow 8 to 10 inches tall. The crinkly outer leaves are a very deep green.

It is slow to bolt and has a stronger resistance to mildew problems than does Parris Island Cos. The flavor of Valmaine is very good indeed, and it is particularly fine in Caesar salads because the savoyed leaves hold the dressing well. Valmaine is generally sown early in the spring and thinned to 8 inches apart to allow the heads to develop, but it can be used in the young leaf stage with continuous sowings from April to August for new leaf salads.

T he crisphead lettuces have the least vitamins in the whole salad group. Cos, or romaine lettuce, has about six times more vitamin A, and three times more calcium than crisphead. Butterhead lettuces have four times as much iron as the crisphead types.

LOBJOIT'S GREEN is an English cos that is much used as a new leaf salad crop with continuous sowings to keep the supply coming, but it can also be grown to maturity, of course. It is a good variety for growing under cloches as many English gardeners do. BARCAROLLE is a big, tall, deep green cos that is a vigorous grower and was highly recommended to English gardeners in the 1977 Wisley Lettuce Trials. ERTHEL CRISP MINT (65 to 80 days) is another English cos with a broad, savoy-type leaf, much rippled and bubbled. It is a sweet, crisp cos that is very slow to bolt (as are most cos lettuces) and can be grown quite densely—6 inches apart, 8 inches between rows. It is tolerant of mildew and mosaic. This is another new leaf salad favorite with English gardeners who sow it continuously for a steady supply. LITTLE GEM or SUGAR COS is an English dwarf cos with a brittle, crisp heart. It rarely grows taller than 6 inches and is about the same width. There is an old French cultivar—ROMAINE BALLON DE BOUGIVAL—that sounds equally short and wide, mentioned in Louis Flament's *Les Salades,* part of a French gardening series published at the turn of the century. Little Gem has leaves of a medium green, which have a blistered appearance. The taste is quite sweet, and some growers rate it the best flavored cos of them all. Little Gem won an award in the 1977 Wisley Lettuce Trials in England.

Intermediate Cos

Crosses between lettuce species and cultivars are nothing new, but there are a few that deserve special attention. Wallop, offered by Thompson and Morgan as a novelty, is a big intermediate that is a cross between a crisphead and a cos. The result is a lettuce with a large, stout head that can weigh as much as one and a half pounds, enough for a really big salad. It is a tender lettuce that is so crisp it almost crackles, but with a fuller flavor than any crisphead type ever claimed. For gardeners who enjoy the texture of crisphead and want the rich taste of cos, this is a good one to try. WINTER DENSITY from England is a cross between a butterhead and a cos, with a sweet, delicate butterhead flavor and a crisp, cos-type leaf. Everyone I know who has tried it has made it a permanent member of the vegetable garden family. It is a superior lettuce, but must be cloched if you try to grow it in the cool spring or autumn seasons. Gardeners with mild climates can try to plant in late summer and then winter it over for early spring crops.

Loose-Leaf Lettuce (*Lactuca sativa* var. *crispa*)

The loose-leaf lettuces are a heterogeneous group distinguished by the loose, nonheading rosette of leaves they form. Some of the leaves of lettuces in this group are very curly and frilly. Some of the brightest stars in the lettuce firmament are loose-leaf types. Two very popular cultivars are GRAND RAPIDS and BLACK-SEEDED SIMPSON. Grand Rapids is very popular both with commercial growers and home gardeners, but is more of an eye pleaser than a palate treat. It is a rapidly maturing lettuce (45 days) with light green leaves, tender and crisp, but without much flavor. The light clear green leaves are frilly and deeply cut on the edges—making a beautiful lettuce. The rapid development and tolerance of adverse conditions, as well as its space-saving habit of not minding close planting, means it comes close to a never-fail lettuce. It is a greenhouse favorite too, one of the best for situations with low light intensities. SLO-BOLT (48 days) is a Grand Rapids type that stands the heat fairly well and is a good summer lettuce. The plants are not consistent in color, with some fairly dark ones among the general light greens. A somewhat mosaic-resistant Slo-Bolt is available from Harris Seeds. WALDMANN'S DARK GREEN (45 days) is a commercial Grand Rapids strain that is darker in color, and with larger, heavier leaves than the rest of the group. Like the others, the edges are ruffled and frilled. Waldmann's is often grown in greenhouses.

There is a handsome engraving of the Black-Seeded Simpson in my 1895 copy of Peter Henderson's *Gardening for Pleasure*. This cultivar has been around for a long time, and like many of the heirloom varieties, it has been popular for more than a century. Black-Seeded Simpson is still a wonderful lettuce, a rapid-growing, very early lettuce with broad frilled and ruffled leaves like the ruching on the cuffs of an eighteenth century dandy, and of a beautiful lime-green color that is striking against the dark soil after a rain. It has a tender, silky texture and a most delicate flavor. It is often grown in cold frames for the earliest crops (45 days). Almost every seed catalog offers this good old lettuce.

GREEN ICE (45 days) is a comparatively new lettuce, a Burpee exclusive, and "the first plant seed product ever to receive a plant patent." Shepherd Ogden of The Cook's Garden in Vermont raises up to 50 European and domestic lettuces for the carriage trade, and he chooses Green Ice as one of his best lettuces. "I love the stuff," he says. It is a shiny dark green color, crisp in texture, and with wavy, fringed, savoyed leaves and a memorable flavor. In addition, it holds well as the summer heat increases.

PRIZE HEAD (sometimes called ALL CREAM) is another old-timer, a very beautiful lettuce with crinkly bronze outer leaves edged in pink and a cream-colored heart in a tender rosette. Last summer I planted 28 lettuce cultivars the day before I left on a three-week trip. While I was gone, I was disturbed by the news of a long, hot dry spell back home that had probably baked my garden into a desert. When I returned, I found that none of the lettuces had been able to weather the drought—except Prize Head, which valiantly offered some small, varicolored leaves to me. They were bitter, of course.

One of the finest lettuces in the loose-leaf group is the French REINE DES GLACES, a deep green lettuce with small, loose heads, the leaves twisted and tweaked on the edges. I have grown it for several years and prize it above all others in my salad garden. It holds well in the heat and has a distinctive and superior flavor. Shepherd Ogden, Vermont's best lettuce grower, remarks, "I have always asked friends and relatives traveling abroad to bring back seeds, and my French brother-in-law brought me Reine des Glaces from two different seed houses a few years ago. I love it, both for the taste, which is almost candylike in comparison to my main-crop varieties, and because it looks so unusual." Reine is a good variety to pick the outer leaves from during the summer and urge the plant to produce more. It makes a beautiful pot plant for the housebound gardener. Several of the import seed houses carry it.

Suddenly there are red lettuces everywhere—RED FIRE, RUBY, and RED SALAD BOWL. Of these, Ruby is an All-America Winner and a spectacular lettuce whose bright green frilly leaves are edged with red color ranging from a deep ruby to a soft pink sunset. Some plants are entirely red. It is a sweet, crisp, tender, and dramatic at the table. Like the other loose leafs, Ruby is a speedy grower, reaching maturity in 47 days. The plant is slow to bolt, and eager gardeners can pick the young leaves as they are ready, keeping the plant producing for three or four weeks. Some gardeners have had success with Ruby as a cut-and-come-again crop, cutting the leaves off when the plant is young for a new leaf salad, and letting the plant force a second crop.

SALAD BOWL is another All-America Winner and it has shot to the top of the lettuce hit charts very rapidly. Developed by the United States Department of Agriculture (USDA) Salad Bowl is a big, loose, very attractive frilly rosette that literally fills a large salad bowl. The leaves are fairly tender, and the flavor is good if not outstanding. There is a green strain and a dark maroon strain. Both colors are capturing a place in gourmet produce departments with their striking good looks. The plants stand hot weather well and take their time about bolting. One of the best ways to grow Salad Bowl is to pick the outer leaves of the plant through the season and let the inner rosette keep on producing. Salad Bowl makes a most ornamental and edible flower bed edging, and it is a knockout pot plant, especially when set on a stand.

OAK LEAF is a very ancient lettuce, centuries old and found on many old lists of salad plants. It grows in a rosette, and the deeply lobed dark leaves do resemble ambitious oak leaves. A century ago in France, there was a bronze-leaved strain called ÄRTICHOKE LEAF, but this seems to have disappeared. Oak Leaf is often grown as a novelty and to add interest to the salad bowl. It can be harvested for a long season by picking the outer leaves and letting the plant produce more. ROYAL OAK LEAF is a Burpee

Once in a while a seed catalog offers something in the lettuce section called Chicken Lettuce (Lactuca sativa var. secalina). This is sometimes grouped with the loose-leaf lettuces and sometimes allowed a category to itself, L. sativa var. secalina. It produces leaves on a stem 3 to 4 feet tall, and while the leaves are certainly edible, the flavor is not as subtle as we like in our salads. You can try it, and if you like it, it's all well and good. Chickens and rabbits, as the popular name suggests, find it most delectable. It is a good leaf producer and keeps making new growth as mature leaves are stripped off. It seems to take a lot out of the soil, and if you grow it, work it into a good crop rotation schedule.

exclusive (50 days) that is heat resistant, has a thick midrib, and makes a large rosette. This strain replaces Burpee's older Oak Leaf.

DEER TONGUE lettuces, once fairly common in our catalogs, have all but disappeared. Shepherd Ogden is the only source I know for MATCHLESS DEER TONGUE lettuce. He remembers it growing in his father's garden. "It is a very beautiful lettuce, dark green and succulent like Buttercrunch, but with a much more interesting leaf form. The leaves are triangular in shape, but take a 90-degree turn in the middle and so form a pinwheellike rosette." Deer tongue lettuces of the old stock are a cool-season crop and will bolt in the summer heat.

DUNSEL is a very swift-growing, round-leaved lettuce from Europe. Its small, very tender yellow green leaves can be harvested four or five weeks after the seed is sown. This is probably the fastest-growing lettuce on the market and gives you something for the salad bowl before other plants have barely germinated.

Growing Lettuce

Rich, well-manured, sandy loam worked to a fine tilth and fat with organic material is paradise for the lettuces, though they can make it on almost any soil that gets enough water. Grand Rapids even prefers a heavy clay soil. A pH tending toward neutral (6.0 to 7.0) suits lettuce best, and an acid soil should be corrected with fine wood ash before growing time.

More important than soil texture and constitution is moisture. Lettuces *must* grow rapidly to be good, and to grow rapidly they need a steady supply of moisture. Serious gardeners know it is madness to depend on the quixotic nature of rainfall. Some sort of regular, sufficient moisture supply is absolutely essential to growing the finest lettuces, whether buckets of water lugged by hand or a trickle irrigation system. Lettuces that are short-changed on water grow slowly, toughen, become bitter, and bolt at the first breath of hot weather. All but a few lettuces resent being crowded by their fellows or by weeds, and they respond to the threat with slow growth and disagreeable bitterness.

The older lettuce varieties take more care to grow. These should be grown rapidly before the weather turns hot, but some of the newer products of the breeder's bench such as Zomerkonig, All the Year Round, Summer Bibb, Augusta, Mission, Webb's Wonderful, and others can mature in summer heat without an appreciable loss of quality.

There are three major sins committed in the lettuce patch. As mentioned above, the first, and most serious, is the failure of the gardener to supply the lettuces with adequate water. If you know you cannot keep your lettuces supplied with water to their taste you are better off giving the seed to a gardening friend who can. It is disappointing and discouraging to prepare the ground, sow the seed, forget to water, and find that very little germinates and nothing grows.

The second sin is failure to sow fresh seed every ten days or so for a continuous supply of prime lettuce. Some gardeners plant only once and expect the garden to produce perfect vegetables all through the summer. The reality is that you will be eating the best lettuce six to eight weeks after you planted it, and around the time the tomatoes are ripe, all the lettuce has gone to seed unless you continued to sow.

The third sin is a failure to thin out the plants properly. From the time lettuce seedlings get their first true leaves they must have plenty of room. Their leaves should never touch those of a neighbor. Large lettuces like Hilde or Salad Bowl may take up 15 to 18 inches of space between plants. Tom Thumb and

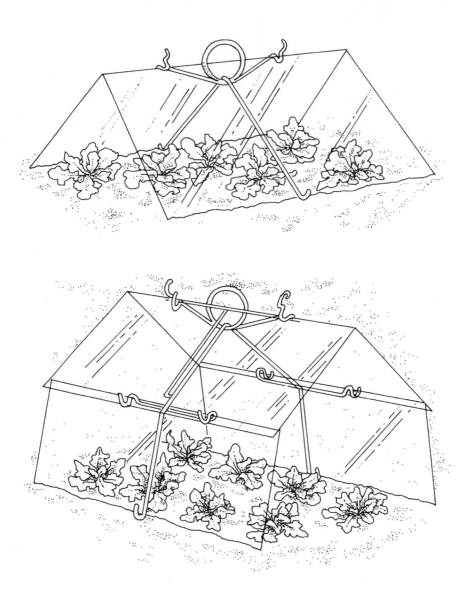

Cloches are a must for serious lettuce growers. Two of the most effective designs are the tent cloche, *top*, and the large barn cloche, *bottom*. Both consist of glass panels held together with wire. The tent cloche has a spring handle with extensions that allow for extra ventilation. The large barn cloche is ideal for taller plants, and the roof glass can be adjusted or removed for ventilation without affecting the stability of the whole unit.

other dwarf lettuces can, of course, be grown much closer together. If you are one of those tender-hearted gardeners who wince at the thought of pulling up eagerly straining, healthy young seedlings just because they are too close together, reflect for a few moments on their fate if you do not thin—spindly, weak plants that are undersized and malnourished, heads that fail to form, and rosettes that do not take shape. Harden your heart and thin them out. If you keep chickens, they will take care of the problem for you and convert the surplus seedlings into eggs and tasty drumsticks.

Lettuce ranks among the top five vegetables in popularity, and it is grown year-round by determined gardeners, even those who live in the North. It can be grown in pots and window boxes, in cold frames and hotbeds, in greenhouses and sunspaces, under cloches and plastic in the garden, and almost any place you can find a patch of soil. Even a small family can dispose of 400 lettuces a year, and with careful planning and the use of season extenders, you can grow a good deal of it at home.

A helpful trick for successful lettuce growing is to start the seed in flats or jiffy pots indoors—somewhere you can control the temperature. If you start seed in your flats indoors all through the season every ten days, you will have a constant supply of lettuce from early spring to early winter, even in the North. It is especially helpful to start lettuce seed inside in midsummer, for the seed does not germinate well at soil temperatures above 68°F, and the upper layer of garden soil dries out very rapidly at this season.

If you don't already use cold frames, cloches, and hotcaps, lettuce production will lead you into it, for these crops do very well in chilly weather with a little protection. The cold frame can give you tender homegrown lettuces in April and October, when other gardeners are glumly eating salads made of supermarket bowling-ball lettuce.

Hardened-off lettuce transplants should go into the garden as soon as the soil is ready to be worked, usually about two weeks before the erratic spring frosts are over. Lettuce is a half-hardy plant that is quite tolerant of light frosts (some botanists think it originated at high altitudes in the dim dark past) and chilly breezes, but if a hard frost threatens, the young plants should be protected. There are three ways to have your transplants ready to go out into the garden in early spring: first, start the seed

A plastic tunnel provides durable, easy-to-assemble, and inexpensive frost protection for early spring lettuce seedlings. Simply bend heavy wire hoops and push them firmly into the ground. Then stretch polyethylene sheeting over the wire hoops, making sure that the plastic touches the soil on both sides. You can hold down the edges of the plastic with stakes or metal hooks.

indoors four to six weeks before transplant time and then harden off the young plants in a cold frame for ten days before setting them out in the garden; or second, sow the seed outside in a cold frame or hotbed four to six weeks before transplant time; or third, you may sow seed directly in the garden bed under cloches or plastic tunnels. (You may need to warm the soil for a week or ten days first with a sheet of clear plastic.) Always keep the young plants ruthlessly thinned, or they will be pathetically undersized and too weak to cope with open garden conditions. Of these three approaches, I find the flat-to-cold-frame-to-garden scenario is the most flexible and produces the best lettuces.

Because lettuce has a fairly shallow root system, it is at the mercy of the conditions in the upper few inches of soil for sustenance; everything in a lettuce's life revolves around sufficient moisture. A light mulch following a good soaking will hold moisture in the soil.

Lettuce beds should be rotated yearly to avoid fungal and bacterial diseases. Leaf lettuces and dwarf cos or butterheads can be interplanted with slow-growing, late-maturing crops such as tomatoes or brussels sprouts. If you are growing lettuce cultivars that suffer in the heat, a few extra days of cool weather can be gained by planting them on the shady side of corn, staked tomatoes, or a row of pole beans. Many gardeners shade their lettuce with muslin or nylon cloth as the summer presses in relentlessly.

It is a good idea to know what season your lettuce cultivars do best in—some have been bred for early spring production, others to take hot weather for long spells, and some to withstand long periods of cold (the so-called winter lettuces that are protected over winter with an eye toward the earliest spring crop). The best seed companies here and almost all European seed com-

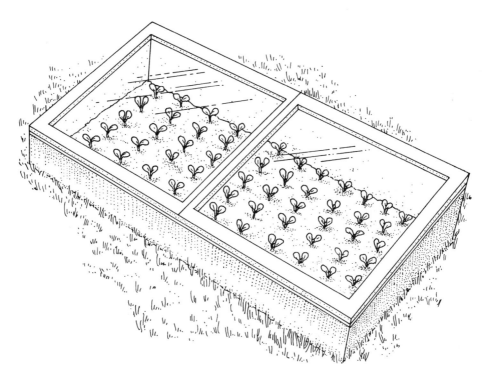

The traditional cold frame makes a fine intermediate home for early spring lettuces after they have outgrown seedling flats and before garden conditions are suitable for permanent transplanting. This simple wood frame has a removable glass cover (an old storm window does nicely), which can be removed for ventilation on warm days and replaced during cool nights.

panies identify lettuce cultivars as "spring," "summer," or "winter" plants.

Harvesting Lettuce

Most garden vegetables are harvested when they are mature or ripe. But there are many ways to harvest lettuce. You can, of course, cut the plants when their heads or rosettes are full and plump, the traditional approach to the salad bowl. But there is a growing movement here as well as abroad in the wake of commercial lettuce growing innovations, to get higher yields and more efficient use of the soil by other harvesting techniques. Certain lettuces lend themselves to these approaches and are divided into gathering lettuces and cut-and-come-again lettuces.

The special cut-and-come-again cultivars have a tendency to especially rapid growth and the ability to resprout vigorously if the stalk is cut just above ground level. Earlier in the century, cutting lettuces were very popular, and many are still grown on the Continent. Strains of BLOND À COUPER (WHITE CUTTING LETTUCE) are commonly used for early cold-frame crops. The first crop of some of these lettuces is ready to harvest only 25 days after sowing, and as many as two successive crops can follow from the cut stumps. Continental home gardeners usually limit production to two crops only out of fear of exhausting the soil. The only true cut-and-come-again lettuce I have found listed in our seed catalogs was Epicure's brief offering of FEUILLE DE CHÊNE BLONDE (47 days) from France, but the following year it had been dropped from the lettuce section. This is much grown in Provence and is very good mixed with young rocket and other early salad crops, including baby Oakleaf. Feuille de Chêne Blonde has deeply indented, pale green leaves and a good flavor. Good gardeners who understand crop rotation and soil building might like to keep an eye out for the cutting lettuces, especially when traveling abroad.

Cut-and-come-again lettuces are harvested when the leaves are about 4 inches tall, and the stump is left above the soil line for the future crops. A dressing of good compost should be worked in around the plants between crops. It is a good idea to give the bed over to a restorative cover crop after the last harvest, because such forced crops take a lot out of the soil. This is not a beginning gardener's technique but might be useful for the experienced old hand who is short of space and who will bring the soil back to good condition after the harvest. Check with the local Cooperative Extension Service for the best cover crops for your area and gardening needs.

---

*R*osalind *Creasy, in* The Complete Book of Edible Landscaping *(1982), suggests using lettuces for edging flower beds and borders, planting them in containers for a striking effect, and mixing them through the flower bed with colorful short flowers, herbs, and other vegetables.*

Gardeners who go abroad and look for these lettuces or who take foreign seed catalogs should remember that in Germany they are called *Schnittsalat;* in France, *à couper;* and in Italy, *da taglio.* Stay-at-home gardeners might like to experiment with domestic loose-leaf types to discover cut-and-come-again talents. In England, the National Vegetable Research Station has tested many loose-leaf lettuces for resprout potential. They found that the young leaves of most lettuces were too bitter to enjoy but that cos lettuces performed well (Erthel Crisp Mint, Paris White, Valmaine, and Lobjoit's Green were named) and so did some of the butterheads (Hilde, Cobham Green, and others). Shepherd Ogden has tried cut-and-come-again tricks with domestic lettuces and is not encouraging. He writes:

> First, the handling of loose leaves is very labor intensive; second, the keeping quality is greatly reduced; third, the wait for second growth seems as wasteful as the wait for seed to germinate and get to the seedling stage; and fourth, the quality of each successive cutting is inevitably lower in my experience—though I have not tried any of the European varieties supposedly bred for cutting.

On the other hand, gathering lettuces are all around us. Most of the loose-leaf types that grow in rosettes respond to the technique of harvesting only the outer leaves of the plant while leaving the center to expand and keep a continuous crop coming. Salad Bowl is a gathering lettuce, though seed catalog illustrations usually show it harvested in its full-bodied splendor. Many gathering lettuces are grown in England and Europe. Joy Larkcom lists several in her column for the Royal Horticultural Society's journal, *The Garden,* including CURLED AUSTRALIAN, CURLED AMERICAN, OAK LEAVED SALAD BOWL, a hardy small Italian type from the Piedmont called LATUGA PARELLA, and an overblown "outstandingly pretty lettuce" LATTUGHINO LOLLO BIONDO. She remarks, "I believe there are also red and yellow forms of Oak Leaved Salad Bowl. It is one of the lettuces used for its ornamental effect in the famous Villandry gardens. There they found that if the central leaves of the plant were cut, the outer green leaves would redden." Both Reine des Glaces and Ruby are also good gathering lettuces.

Winter Lettuce

Winter lettuces are not often grown here, but they are worth a try if you think your climate is right. Traditionally they are sown in September in a bed of fine soil and then transplanted to a cold frame when the hard frosts begin to threaten. They are *gradually* mulched deeper and deeper in the frames as the cold increases. A good heavy snowfall might ensure their well-being, but intense cold with no snow cover would mean disaster. In England, Belgium, and France, where winter lettuces are standard crops, the cold frame and heavy mulching are enough to carry the plants through. In April the procedure is reversed. Now the mulch is gradually drawn off the plants, and the shelter of the frame encourages growth in the dormant lettuces. By the end of April, a rapid spurt of renewed vigor has brought the lettuces up to the first harvest of the year.

I recently had a letter from a lettuce grower in England, Mr. R. J. Tebbit in Essex who has grown thousands of winter lettuces. His procedure is to seed in the open bed in September and again in October if the germination rate was poor. From the end of November until Christmas, he transplants the seedlings 9 inches apart and 10 inches between rows. Any blank places in his rows are filled before the end of December. The plants get no protection whatsoever through the winter. The cultivar is IMPERIAL, a winter lettuce Mr. Tebbit has been growing for 40 years. In March, he waters with a liquid fertilizer along the rows, hoes it in gently and pulls out any weeds. The tiny plants—only about two inches across—expose little leaf surface to the elements, but their root systems are large and well established. By the end of April, the rows are literally filled with a sea of large, glistening, light green lettuces. The money from the sale of Mr. Tebbit's crop has been donated toward the county's purchase of a cancer scanner.

*B*eginning gardeners make two common errors with lettuce: One, they plant too much seed early in the season and none at all later on, so that there is a surplus and then a dearth of the leafy green stuff. And two, they transplant lettuce seedlings too late. Young lettuce plants should be set out in the garden when only an inch tall. Protect them if the weather is still unsettled.

Mr. Tebbit's system will not work in climates where snow falls, for moisture that gets inside the folded leaves causes the hearts to rot. Gardeners in snowless regions might like to buy Imperial or other winter lettuce seed from overseas suppliers and experiment. Our catalogs do list a few winter lettuce imports. VAL D'ORGE from Belgium is a specialty of the famous Gonthier seedhouse. It makes large, blond green heads very resistant to cold and should be carried through the winter by either of the systems described above. Epicure lists Val d'Orge in its catalog. ARCTIC KING is listed in the catalog of Thompson and Morgan as a winter lettuce with a large head and light green crinkled leaves. I must admit that I have not yet tried to nurse winter lettuce through a Vermont winter, which can stretch from October through May in a bad year, although if the lettuces were under cover and well mulched, and a good snowfall insulated the earth early in the season, it might be possible to do so. There are three quite famous over-winter lettuces in Europe known as

"The Three Ks"—KNAP, KLOEK, and KWIEK. The seed for these lettuces is sown early in October in the Low Countries, much as Mr. Tebbit does, and they mature in April. Knap is reputed to be an outstanding April lettuce, though the seed has not appeared in our catalogs.

Gardeners in cold climates who cannot bring winter lettuces through can still enjoy autumn-harvested lettuces. This is a most pleasing crop. Gardeners all around you might be hanging up their hoes and making the reluctant switch from homegrown to store bought, but you can still be gathering beautiful salad crops that are just coming into perfection, their flavors improved with the subtle sweet nuttiness that the first chill weather brings to them. The early, cool-weather lettuces and the short-season types do well at this late day. Tests at the Wisley Lettuce Trials with autumn-maturing lettuces distilled fine drops of wisdom for would-be growers. In England the seeds for autumn harvested lettuces are sown around August tenth. Patrick Walker describes this in *The Garden* (August 1975):

> Rather than stuff the soil with bulky organic matter for this sowing, rely on the residues ensuing from a site given generous treatment earlier in the year. . . . After ensuring that the soil is thoroughly moist, seed is sown in clusters in the open ground; each cluster being spaced 8½ inches apart each way. After germination eliminate all but the most robust specimen at each station. Visual comparison at Wisley between trial plants sown in this way and those subsequently transplanted is invariably in favor of the lettuces which are sown *in situ* and then singled.

My own experiments have shown that in a dry summer it is difficult to get lettuce seed to germinate in the August garden. The soil dries out very rapidly, and the temperature is often too high for good lettuce germination. It is good insurance to start some seed in flats inside as well as in clusters in the garden bed. Shepherd Ogden remarks:

> . . . I don't presently do any direct seeding of lettuce for my production crop—all of my lettuce is transplanted from seedbeds into production beds in the intensive way (not strictly French intensive, but quite similar). Thus I control the conditions in the seedbeds . . . so that the weather doesn't throw off my planting schedule. . . . During the hot dry spell last summer,

I had to cover large portions of my beds with old screens I have collected from the dump to be able to transplant at all for a month.

The thinned lettuces are given every encouragement to make good growth before the days shorten appreciably. As the threat of frost grows closer and closer, the weather is closely watched, and, finally, the lettuces are covered with cloches or a plastic tunnel. The soil should be thoroughly soaked before the covers are set in place. When a hard frost warning comes, cover the cloches with straw mats or mulch or leaves. Alternately, if you have only a few lettuces, you can set the cold frame over them for protection instead of using plastic or cloches. Some northern gardeners have built a north wall with haybales and spread out a cover of plastic that is like a lean-to tent. Storm windows can

A makeshift miniature greenhouse can be made by leaning storm windows against a north wall of haybales. This simple structure is easy to set up on short notice and allows the gardener to carry the lettuce harvest well beyond the first autumn frost.

Nutritional Values of Salad Greens

	Percentage of Water	Calories	Protein (g)	Fat (g)	Carbohydrate (g)	Ash (g)	Calcium (mg)
Chicory: leaf (raw)	92.8	20	1.8	0.3	3.8	1.3	86
Chicory: Witloof (raw)	95.1	15	1.0	0.1	3.2	0.6	18
Dandelion (raw)	85.6	45	2.7	0.70	9.2	1.8	187†
Endive (raw)	93.1	20	1.7	0.1	4.1	1.0	81
Escarole	94	12	1.2	0.2	1.5	...	50
Garden cress (raw)	89.4	32	2.6	0.70	5.5	1.8	81
Lettuce: butterhead	95.1	14	1.2	0.2	2.5	1.0	35
Lettuce: crisphead	95.5	13	0.9	0.1	2.9	0.6	20
Lettuce: loose leaf	94.0	18	1.3	0.3	3.5	0.9	68
Mustard greens (raw)	89.5	31	3.0	0.5	5.6	1.4	183†
Sorrel (raw)	90.0	28	2.1	0.3	5.6	1.1	66
Spinach (raw)	90.7	26	3.2	0.3	4.3	1.5	93
Watercress (raw)	93.3	19	2.2	0.3	3.0	1.2	151

SOURCE: United States Department of Agriculture, *Composition of Food.*
NOTE: The nutritional values given are for 100 grams.
*Outstanding source.
†Good source.

be leaned against the hay bales to make a similar crude greenhouse that will carry the lettuces deep into the frost period.

Once you have learned, by trial and error, what lettuces do well for you, you can plant the known and dependable types as a matter of course and work in more unusual types as experi-

Phosphorus (mg)	Iron (mg)	Sodium (mg)	Potassium (mg)	Vitamin A (I.U.)	Thiamine (mg)	Riboflavin (mg)	Niacin (mg)	Vitamin C (mg)
40	0.9	...	420	4,000*	0.06	0.10	0.5	22†
21	0.5	7	182	trace	...	...	...	...
66	3.1†	76	397	1,400*	0.19†	0.26†	...	35†
54	1.7†	14	294	3,300*	0.07	0.14	0.5	10
21	0.7	72†	240	1,600†	0.09	0.07	0.4	5
76	1.3†	14	606†	9,300*	0.08	0.26†	1.0†	69*
26	2.0†	9	264	970	0.06	0.06	0.3	8
22	0.5	9	175	330	0.06	0.06	0.3	6
25	1.4†	9	264	1,900†	0.05	0.08	0.4	18
50	3.0†	32	377	7,000*	0.11†	0.22†	0.8	97*
41	1.6†	5	338	12,900*	0.09	0.22†	0.5	119*
51	3.1†	71†	470	8,100*	0.10†	0.20†	0.6	51†
54	1.7†	52	282	4,900*	0.08	0.16	0.9†	79†

ments. Try to set up a lettuce succession from early spring to late fall with a number of cultivars. Hilde can be sown very early; a month later sow Lobjoit's Green or Windermere; then any of the heat-resistant sorts that mature in midsummer are great; and follow with the autumn-harvest lettuces.

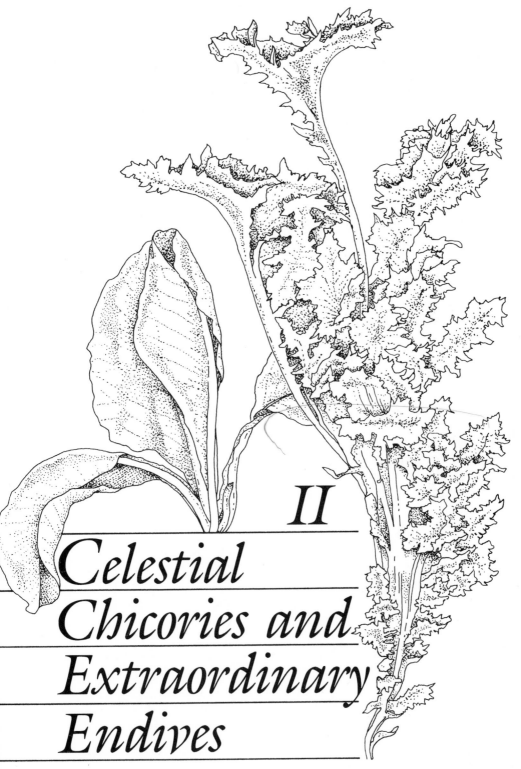

II
Celestial
Chicories and
Extraordinary
Endives

The fascinating chicory species *(Cichorium intybus)* range from wayside weeds to vegetables for cooking, from coffee substitutes to the stuff of superb salads. The plant group, with its charming blue, white, or pink flowers, is amazingly variable. In one form it is a stout perennial that grows from 3 to 6 feet high, but the sorts we usually plant in our gardens are annuals, harvested at every stage of plant development, and come in many flavors, forms, textures, and shapes. The little delicate leaves of some kinds are used straight from the garden; others grow into mounded rosette heads. Still others form conical "sugar loaves" weighing up to 2 pounds. Some chicories are red, some green, some multicolored. Still others are forced in darkness to grow thick little cones called chicons; another forced type sends out fine pale yellow leaves. The Catalogna chicories thrust up clusters of asparaguslike shoots called *puntarelle*.

Chicory, once called succory, probably originated in the Mediterranean area where so many fine salad greens emerged, and it has been a favorite in the salad bowl since ancient days. But chicories are also braised, baked, roasted over glowing coals, and sautéed; they are vegetables of great character, misunderstood and underutilized in this country, and they deserve a place of honor in every gardener's salad garden.

We know that domestic chicories were grown in late medieval gardens, and the estimable John Gerard comments in his great *Herbal* of 1633 that salads of chicory "comfort the weake and feeble stomacke." Chicory was thought to cleanse the blood, act as a spring tonic, bind the bowels, aid cases of jaundice, cure inflamed eyes, and prevent kidney stones. As Queen Elizabeth lay on her death bed, the only food she would take was "succory broth," noted Geoffrey Grigson in his absorbing study, *An Englishman's Flora* (London, 1955).

The chicories were powerful plants in the twilight world of folklore and magic. Margaret Baker has written a curious little book for England's Shire Publications, entitled *Discovering the Folklore of Plants* (1969, 1980). She writes the following about chicory:

> Chicory had the useful power to render the possessor invisible and shared with moonwort the power to open locked boxes if a leaf were held against the lock. For the magic to work it must be picked on St James' Day (25th July) and must be cut

in silence with a golden knife. If the cutter spoke during the work he would die.

I had a neighbor once who was fond of gardening in the nude. Since she lived quite near the road—admittedly it was a back country road—her efforts attracted a certain amount of attention from passersby; she obviously wasn't growing chicory!

Today dozens of chicory cultivars are grown in Europe, especially in Italy where all the chicories are greatly relished, and many regional types have been developed over the centuries. Italian seed catalogs list pages of chicories, and most European seedsmen offer their home garden customers a choice of at least 10 or 12 chicories. Gardeners on this side of the Atlantic are lucky if they can find 3 or 4, and the puzzlement about what is chicory and what is endive has convinced many they are the same. The two are indeed closely related, but there are differences. Still, gardeners and garden writers have been mixing the two up for centuries. John Parkinson in his 1629 *Paradisi in Sole, Paradisus Terrestris* (the title is a pun on Parkinson's name in Latin, no doubt thought very witty in the seventeenth century) dealt briskly with the problem when he wrote:

> I put both Succorie and Endive into one chapter and description, because they are both of one kindred; and although they differ a little the one from the other, yet they agree both in this, that they are eaten eyther greene or whited, of many.

Some modern garden writers think John Parkinson referred to the forced Witloof chicons when he spoke of "whited" chicories and endive, but it is more likely that he meant blanched heads. Blanching salad greens was a very common garden technique from the Middle Ages through the nineteenth century. The discovery of vitamins and their importance in the human diet changed this cultural habit. Giovanni Baptista Porta wrote the entertaining and extremely popular *Magia Naturalis (Natural Magick)* in 1558, and it was rapidly published in many editions in seven languages. He had much to say about growing plants and gives us directions for three methods of blanching endives, chicories, and lettuces. First, one can tie up the leaves with a bit of string to make them "white and tender"; or, one can earth them up to "whiten them by casting sand upon them"; or, one

Blanching is essential for producing creamy, mild-flavored heads of endive or chicory. Shown here are two ways to blanch endive: *top*, carefully tying up the outer leaves with strips of soft cloth or lengths of string; and *bottom*, inverting a large clay pot over the entire plant (and covering the drainage hole in the bottom of the pot). In either case, you may want to check the plants periodically to make sure excess moisture does not build up and cause rotting.

may cover the heads with an overturned earthenware pot. Nowhere is the procedure for forcing chicons described, a bit of natural magic that would have delighted Porta.

Joy Larkcom, whose column, "The Kitchen Garden," is eagerly followed by readers of the Royal Horticultural Society's journal, *The Garden,* divides the confusing tangle of chicories into seven basic (but overlapping) categories: the red leaf, heading, green rosette, cutting, "wild," Catalogna, and Witloof. We can follow these categories of chicories for the sake of clarity, but let the reader be warned that some cultivars appear in several different divisions of types. Chicories are versatile.

The chicories like a rich, well-drained, deeply spaded, weed-free soil, as do the majority of domestic plants. French and Belgian gardeners, who grow very fine chicories, spend much time in the classic gardening posture, preparing beds, shoveling in manure, working in compost, and raking and sieving the soil until it is as fine as flour for their beloved chicories. The plants all mature to perfection in cool weather, and they often benefit from heavy mulching, which cools their roots and keeps moisture in the soil. They do best in gentle climates where there is a long, gently cooling fall and a mild winter; Italy is ideal for the chicories. They can also be successfully grown much farther north, though the gardening techniques will be more rigorous in protecting the plants from hard frosts long enough to let them mature. Perhaps it will even be necessary to move a few select heads into a root cellar to winter over when early spring salads are wanted.

Red-Leaf Chicories

The red chicories are the beautiful regional cultivars from Italy that have no rivals anywhere on earth. They are used in salads, or braised, or roasted over charcoal fires *al fresco* and served with spiced oil and vinegar dressing. These chicories are green when young and during the summer. They turn red only in the fall and winter. The outer leaves of the heading cultivars close tightly around the core when cold weather sets in, making a brilliant red, dense, crisp head. If these chicories are cloched or grown under plastic (as northern gardeners in this country might want to do) the heads will be looser and tend to remain greener than those that take the full onslaught of the cold out in the open. In Italy the most cold-resistant chicories are left in the garden right into the winter. The more delicate are protected with boughs and brushwood that have straw heaped over them. In this country, where winters everywhere but the South are far more severe than the warm Italian climate, gardeners will have to experiment to discover how far into the winter the chicories they grow can make it and how much protection they need. Fortunately, the chicories are a fairly hardy group of plants and can tolerate light frosts when they are young. But in the fall, when they are maturing, they suffer in sudden sharp plunges of the temperature unless they are sheltered.

Joy Larkcom toured Italy studying the chicories a few years ago, and she listed VERONA, CHIOGGIA, TREVISO, CASTEL-FRANCO, and ORCHIDEA ROSSA as the major red-leaved cultivars. No less than three of these have turned up in recent seed catalogs in this country, and Suffolk Herbs, an English seed house, carries almost all of them. Italian seed catalogs, of course, list many more. If you travel abroad, or have friends who are planning a trip to Europe, make this a chance to collect some foreign seed catalogs and even unusual seeds.

RADICCHIO DI TREVISO is available from Le Jardin du Gourmet. This world-renowned chicory is unique to a small area around Verona at the foot of the Dolomites, and it is at its most brilliant when the air is bracing and sharp. Treviso makes a spectacular, rose-red, conical head with sharply defined white veins. During the summer the leaves are a light green, but the plants begin to change color as the temperature drops. This plant is the pride of Treviso, and for a long time it was grown nowhere else in the world. Waverly Root in *The Cooking of Italy,* quotes a local rhyme that goes:

> *Se lo guardi, egli e un sorriso;*
> *Se lo mangi, e un paradiso:*
> *Il radicchio di Treviso!*

Loosely translated, this means, "If you look at it, it makes you smile with pleasure; if you eat it, it is paradise: it is the red chicory of Treviso!"

The roots are sometimes forced to make a tender, more subtly colored leaf. Treviso is one of the least hardy of the red chicories, although a new F_1 hybrid of Treviso is available in Italy that can take lower temperatures. So far it has not appeared in any of our seed catalogs.

The Verona is, by contrast, a very hardy, ball-headed red chicory that matures during the mild Italian winter, but here it can be brought into the root cellar and forced. It is adapted to a slow, steady decline in temperature over a long period of months, and here, where cold autumnal temperatures sometimes fall on us like a wolf on the sheepfold, these chicories perform differently. Left outside, they fail to form the tight solid heads one sees in Italy but produce delicious, looser, only moderately well-colored central leaves in my northern New England garden before severe cold strikes them down. But Sarah and Gary Milek of Windsor, Vermont, 40 miles south of my garden, found that their Verona chicory, grown from seed they bought in Italy, stayed stubbornly green in the autumn garden, despite the dropping thermometer. But, by bringing the plants, roots and all, into the cellar, they were able to get the lively color change in the form of apple-sized little heads of brilliant red and white, for a spectacular series of January and February salads.

Gardeners in the mid-Atlantic and southern states and California may find it easy to mature Verona outside in the garden, but northern gardeners will probably have to experiment to find the right procedures to get the little red heads, starting with cloche and plastic tunnel protection, and resorting, if necessary, to lifting the plants and forcing them in the cellar.

Seed catalogs from abroad occasionally offer several Verona strains—an EARLY VERONA, an intensely scarlet SCARLA, and OMEGA, which has unusually large leaves.

Once in a while, some of our specialty seed catalogs list the beautiful CASTELFRANCO VARIEGATA, a sweeter, milder chicory than the other reds, and shaped like a camellia, all streaked with pink, rose, bronze, and apple green. It is a stunning plant, though less spectacular than the crimson Treviso and Verona. Traditionally, Italian salad fanciers think it is a mistake to mix Castelfranco with the Verona in the same salad bowl on aesthetic grounds, but in practice it happens all the time. Purists keep the two types separate, so each may be appreciated for its unique qualities, without interference from a rival.

Castelfranco is green during the summer and only takes on its marbled hues in the chill of autumn. It is, like the other red chicories, autumnal salad material. This cultivar is reputed not to force well, so northern growers may have trouble bringing it to table.

There is another variegated chicory—Orchidea Rossa—the Red Orchid, grown in Italy and southern European gardens. This cultivar reputedly has meltingly soft colors and soft leaves like a butterhead lettuce. It is delicate in taste, texture, and temperament, and it cannot take abrupt cold weather.

Chioggia is another tender red chicory, grown in Italy almost exclusively in the sandy coastal region below Venice. It is a major winter crop in the area, and many local strains have been developed by families that have grown Chioggia for generations. Winter fields of this cultivar along the roads of the region are a striking sight.

Growing Red Chicories

In Italy, the red chicories are seeded from May to July, which is closer to our June-August section of summer. If they are seeded earlier, the plants will be likely to bolt in the summer heat.

It is not easy to start salad crops from seed directly in the garden in warm summer weather, for the soil dries out and overheats before the seed can germinate or before the little seedlings are well established, unless you are set up for drip irrigation. Many gardeners prefer to start the seeds indoors in flats, or in a cold frame or seedling bed, where temperature and moisture can be controlled, and then transplant to the garden proper when four leaves are developed on the young plants.

When the plants are set out, or thinned, if you have got them started *in situ,* they should be placed 10 to 12 inches apart.

General garden care takes them through to autumn. These tasks include weeding, supplying sufficient moisture, and side dressing the rows or beds if the soil needs it or if you're planting autumn seed for a spring crop on the same patch of ground.

In the fall, as the plants turn red, harvest the chicories by cutting them at ground level, or, if the season is long and mild and you want to try for a few extra leaves, make the cut a little aboveground, leaving a stump, and a few new leaves may be forced.

If your season is short, cover the plants with cloches or a plastic tunnel as the season of killing frosts comes on. The colors will not be as vivid as plants ripened in the open, nor will the heads be as solid, but the harvest will be prolonged. If your gardening activities are halted dead in their tracks by an early winter, you may have to bring the chicories into the root cellar and force them.

Forcing chicories in the cellar is quite similar to forcing Witloof, except that with the red chicories, the leaves are not trimmed away. Use a garden fork to lift the plants without breaking the roots or damaging the heads; two people can do this more expeditiously than one. Tie the leaves up with a bit of string as though you were preparing to blanch the heads—which, in a sense, you are. A temperature of about 55°F is a good one for forcing. Bring the plants into the root cellar and set them in boxes of sand, or directly in the earth, if you prefer, with the roots packed together as tightly as possible. After two weeks, check one of the heads every ten days or so until they are ready—small, tight, red and white heads about the size of an orange. Mix them with other salad greens, especially the late lettuces. These forced chicories have a tender leaf and a nutty, mildly bitter flavor.

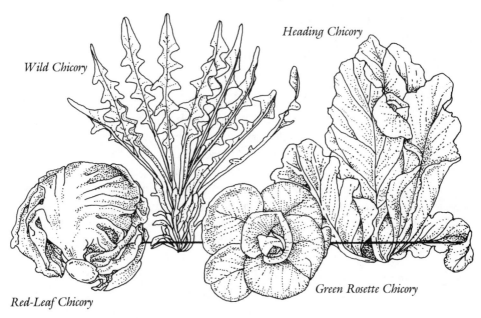

Heading Chicory

Wild Chicory

Green Rosette Chicory

Red-Leaf Chicory

Heading Chicories

Heading chicories are also called Sugar Loaf chicories. They are tall, and shaped quite like Chinese cabbages, with an extremely crispy texture and mild flavors that seem sweet compared to some of the stronger chicories. Suffolk Herbs offers PAN DI ZUCCHERO, sweet and crunchy. It is usually sown in June in England for an autumn harvest, says Joy Larkcom. The plants should be thinned to stand 8 to 10 inches apart as soon as they have developed four leaves. As the summer heat intensifies, the chicory heads benefit from being shaded. Garden and nursery suppliers carry woven polypropylene fabric in several shade densities (50 to 75 percent shade density) for relieving plants from direct sunlight.

BIANCA DI MILANO, or MILAN WHITE, is another Sugar Loaf chicory from Suffolk Herbs. This makes a crisp, long head with white and green leaves. In North America, the Canadian seed house, William Dam, offers us GREENLOF, described as a "Sugar Hat Chicory" and claimed as a new vegetable combining the qualities of endive and Witloof chicory! New, perhaps, on this side of the Atlantic.

The Sugar Loaf chicories are adapted to a mild climate and cannot take much cold. Joy Larkcom remarks that they will bear an English winter if they are protected by a plastic tunnel. Southern and California gardeners here can probably grow these succulent chicories without difficulty, but the northern gardener will have to scramble around and try his or her luck with tall plastic tunnels or high frames covered with plastic.

Growing Heading Chicories

These tall, cylindrical chicories should be started in July in mild climates for a fall harvest. Northern gardeners run the very real risk of never seeing a mature head if they follow this timetable, yet if the chicories are started sooner, they will likely bolt in midsummer heat. Shading the plants in the dog days may prevent bolting, if you want to try starting the chicories earlier. If you decide to plant in July and trust to luck for a mild autumn, give it a go, but be prepared to offer the forming heads some protection if a cold snap comes on. Often, in Vermont, a few days of early-season hard frost is followed by several weeks of Indian summer, so if one can nurse plants through the cold snap, they may mature. This is also true in the mountains of Colorado. Plastic tunnels, cloches, a miniature greenhouse made of a wall of haybales with a few windows leaned up against them, or a tall cold frame that can accommodate the height of these big chicories are some of the tricks you can try.

In Europe, the Sugar Loaf chicories are sometimes sown in the fall to produce an early spring crop, for the young leaves are more tolerant of cold than the big, robust autumn heads. This is a thick sowing of seed on a well-prepared bed in late fall. The young, crowded leaves thrust up in profusion in the early days of spring. Harvest this spring reward by cutting the plants at ground level. Salads made from these baby Sugar Loaf leaves are an expensive delicacy in European restaurants.

Green Rosette Chicories

The rosette chicories lead double lives. In the winter and early spring, they are plump, low mounds of little round leaves that make a delicious and refreshing salad just when greenery is hungered for most acutely. In late spring to autumn, the leaves are long and full and quite bitter, even for the Italian taste, which sends this chicory to the poultry yard during the hot weather, preferring the rosettes for the more delicate salads of winter and early spring.

Growing Green Rosette Chicories

GRUMOLO is an important rosette chicory that is grown in Italy in fine, light soil that is well worked-up, manured, and raked to a fare-thee-well. The seed can be sown in early spring, and as the plant grows through the summer it is cut back once or twice for salads for the chickens, each time leaving a stump about 2 inches high to encourage the rosette shape. As the cool autumn approaches, the gardener stops cutting the plants and they are left to themselves, standing out in the open all winter. By the very earliest spring days they are transformed into rosette heads of tender round leaves that are cut for market or table. These chicories are quite hardy.

Both Grumolo and GRUMOLO INVERNALE DI MILANO (Milan Winter Grumolo) are available from Suffolk Herbs. They may both be sown thickly on a prepared bed in autumn or early, early spring and used as cutting salads when the leaves are a few inches high.

It will be difficult for northern gardeners to have early spring salads from Grumolo unless they mulch the plants as winter approaches or have good snow cover early in the season. Italian market gardeners, says Joy Larkcom, plant in August and cover the plants with plastic as winter draws on for a January harvest. If the plants are left in the open there, they develop much more slowly and are not ready for gathering until March, the traditional spring salad time in this Mediterranean country. Larkcom suggests that English gardeners might want to try intercropping Grumolo with other fall harvest crops, such as cabbage, or, starting Grumolo in the cool shade and shelter of corn or pea vines, then remaining *in situ* after the corn and peas have been harvested.

When rosette chicories bolt and flower, the imaginative Italian salad gardener adds the blossoms to the salad bowl.

Cutting Chicories

The idea of cutting chicories and cutting lettuces sounds odd to us, and it is not the aim of any plant breeder I know to select for good cutting leaf characteristics on this side of the Atlantic. The idea is to sow seed lavishly in a prepared bed, then harvest the seedlings when they are only a few inches tall, then let the plants grow again for a second harvest, or sometimes even a third. North American gardeners wonder, Why not let the plants grow to a good size before harvesting them? The answer lies in the extremely tender texture and the ethereal taste sensations these young salads provoke. The idea is not *just* salads, but *exquisite* salads. The little leaves are not bland; some are tangy, some sharp, some slightly bitter, but each has a characteristic taste.

Head and rosette chicories and many of the red chicories can be treated as cutting chicories by sowing them early in the spring and taking the first harvest while the plants are small. The Sugar Loaf types are often sown in the fall and cut in early spring as a seasonal delicacy.

SPADONA is a special cutting chicory grown for a continuous flush of salad leaves. The name Spadona means "broadsword" and the large narrow leaves have a long, swordlike shape. It is sown in the Piedmont section of Italy from March to September every few weeks or so and is cut twice a month at the height of the season. It needs plenty of water and fertilizer and compost side dressing to keep on producing so abundantly, and it can exhaust a soil if the gardener is not conscientious. Spadona leaves are picked, bundled together, and tied in neat stacks for the Italian markets through late winter and early spring. The winter crops are grown in greenhouses for appreciative consumers.

Growing Cutting Chicories

The general procedure for growing cutting chicories is outlined above, but gardeners who try for these single-leaf crops can plant them in beds, rows, or even indoors in large pots or interior window boxes filled with rich soil. Spadona enjoys regular shots of manure tea. I have kept a barrel of water in the garden for years and dump in rabbit or horse manure from time to time. There is always a rich supply of this plant elixir at hand, and the chicories are especially grateful for it.

Wild Chicory

The so-called *chicorée sauvage* grown in France and Italy is actually a cultivar named BARBE DE CAPUCHIN ("Capuchin Monk's Whiskers"). The seed is offered in this country by Le Jardin du Gourmet. Grown in the garden, this is a distinctly bitter plant for which one must acquire a taste. On the Continent it is usually chopped fine and used sparingly with other salad greens if it is used at all in its green state. It is more commonly a forced winter vegetable, and the delicious, crisp, pale and wispy leaves have a delicate nutty flavor that is only faintly bitter. L. H. Bailey's 1914 *Cyclopedia of Horticulture* offers good directions for forcing Barbe de Capuchin:

> For Barbe, the roots are laid horizontally in tiers on moist earth, the whole forming a sloping heap, the crowns of the roots protruding an inch or so. Since darkness is essential, a warm vegetable cellar is the usual place selected to grow this vegetable which requires three or four weeks to produce its fine white leaves. These are cut when about 6 inches long, eaten as salad . . . or cut up like slaw. If undisturbed, the roots will continue to produce for several weeks.

Growing and Forcing Wild Chicory

Louis Flament of the *Ecole Nationale d'Horticulture de Versailles,* has a good deal to say about the culture of Barbe and begins seven or eight months before the salad is wanted, with a description of preparing the bed and enriching the soil where the roots, from which the forced "whiskers" will spring, are to be nourished. A strong, lusty root is all important for forcing Barbe. The seed is sown from the first two weeks in April to early June. The soil should be of good quality, deeply worked, and fairly new to the game of growing things. (One assumes he means the soil should not be exhausted or overworked by previous crops. Today's gardener practices soil building after a heavy-feeding crop.) The rows should be spaced far enough apart to allow easy hoeing and weeding. During the summer, it is good for strong root production to cut back the plants to within 3 or 4 inches of ground level. The leaves can be fed to livestock.

In October or November the time has arrived to begin the forcing process. One lifts the plants out of the garden and looks them over carefully. Those with weak or small or defective roots are discarded. The large, strong ones have all their leaves removed except for the central bud, which must be left intact. If there are a great many to be done, says Louis Flament, the work goes faster if the leaves are pulled off with a slight twisting motion.

When the sorting and deleafing process is over, roots of the same diameter are bundled together, the bundles are tied up with a twist of osier (string will do very nicely), and the tips of the bundled roots trimmed to the same length. Now the gardener has neatly packaged bundles of roots of the same size and same length. They are ready for the specially prepared forcing bed.

The forcing bed should be in a clean root cellar that is dark and not too large, for a certain amount of warmth is crucial to the best Barbe. The bed is essentially a hotbed, with at least a foot of soil atop plenty of fresh hot manure that will generate sufficient heat to force the "whiskers." Too large a cellar will allow the precious heat to dissipate. The soil over the manure is lightly sprinkled with water, and the bundles of roots are laid on it. Any spaces between the bundles are filled with a little compost or old rotted manure. Now the heap is given a good sprinkling, and the cellar is closed up. In a little while the chicories will start to force their vegetation. Now it will be necessary to sprinkle the pile again, but not too much—better light, frequent sprinklings than heavy, occasional wettings. To judge the right amount of water is a business of experience—the hotter the bed, the more water is needed. Overwatering can lead to mildew and leaf rot.

Eighteen to twenty-five days after the roots were laid on the hotbed, the Barbe should be ready for harvest. The leaves will be tender, faintly bitter, and of a beautiful amber yellow color. They will be about 7 to 10 inches long. The bundles are lifted out, taken apart, and made into smaller bundles ready for market.

It would be interesting to try Barbe production using a heat cable under the bed instead of fresh manure. Flament calls for a temperature ". . . de 20° a 25°," which translates on my thermometer 68 to 77°F. The heat cable, which could produce steady, constant heat, might allow better ventilation and decrease the chance of mildew or rot.

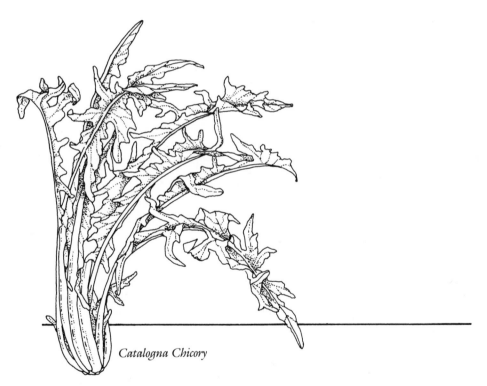

Catalogna Chicory

Catalogna Chicories

Catalogna chicories come either as large-leaved cooking types, or as the asparagus Catalognas that push up tender, pale shoots from the earth in early spring. These *puntarelle,* as they are called, are eaten fresh in salads or cooked. Stokes Seeds lists an asparagus type of "Cicoria Catalogna," but does not give a cultivar name. Joy Larkcom comments on these shoots "that only certain varieties—CATALOGNA PUGLIESE and CATALOGNA PUNTARELLA . . . form these shoots in spring and early summer." These are grown mostly in southern Italy, and demand a mild winter, so their range in this country will be restricted to southern gardeners, who may still have a little trouble. But it's worth the effort to a gardener with an inquiring mind and a jaded palate.

Growing Catalogna Chicories

The *puntarelle* types are sown in autumn in Italy, and before the winter sets in, are transplanted 15 inches apart. Over the mild Mediterranean winter the plants are quiescent, but in the spring they send up a large central stalk that will bear flowers if left to its own devices. The gardener, however, comes with a pruning knife and cuts the stalk away at the base. The plant then puts its all into throwing up many replacement shoots, the so-called *puntarelle,* or "points," which look like little asparagus emerging from the soil in a mass. These are very tender and delicious if cut at once while they are still young. If they are not harvested early they will be hollow and woody in texture. They are used raw in salads, or sometimes cooked as are Witloof chicons. This luxurious salad is hardly known to North Americans, except to travelers who visit Italy in the spring.

Witloof Chicories

There are a number of large-rooted chicories, most of them the cultivars that make the coffeelike beverage without caffeine. German gardeners have developed two of the best kinds, named after the towns that specialized in growing them—MAGDEBURG and BRUNSWICK. PALINGHOP is another large-rooted chicory, and there are several Italian types, including SONCINO and CHIAVARI, which are also regional delicacies. All of these may be cooked and served as vegetables, despite the bitter taste in both roots and leaves. In Italy, the roots are cooked, sliced, and left to stand in a marinade of vinegar before they are added to salads. When the roots are intended for chicory "coffee," the plants are grown to encourage maximum root size. They are harvested in the fall by forking them out of the ground, cutting off the leaves and letting the roots dry in the sun for a few hours. A soft brush cleans the roots off thoroughly, and then they are cut in small pieces, laid on a cookie sheet, and roasted at low heat in the oven until they are a dark brown color and very brittle. They can be stored in covered jars until wanted, then ground in a coffee mill or food grinder, or stored away already ground. Many seed houses offer Magdeburg, and a few, Brunswick. The roots can be raised easily in northern Vermont gardens and should present little difficulty to gardeners in other parts of the country who enjoy chicory.

The Witloof chicories also belong to the large-rooted crowd. Salad lovers who garden eventually find themselves involved with the forcing types of roots, for many of the most toothsome salad delicacies are grown this way. The prince of them all is the famous Witloof chicory whose roots produce the delectable chicons, prized for their ineffable table merits rather than their nutritional qualities.

There are several stories told about the discovery of chicons. Barbara Norman in her *Tales of the Table* (1972) tells us that these treasures were unknown until 1850. The story goes that in that year the head gardener of the Belgian Horticultural Society had some chicory plants in a dark basement and noticed that if they were earthed up, they grew a tight-furled, cream-colored hard cone of leaves that made extraordinarily fine eating. Joy Larkcom's version involves an unknown Belgian farmer who tossed some chicory roots he had grown for coffee use into a dark shed and forgot about them. When he discovered them some time later, they had metamorphosed into crisp, succulent chicons, and one of Belgium's great agricultural crops developed from the fortuitous accident. However, evidence from old gardening books hints that the Low Countries had forced endive before the nineteenth century. J. C. Loudon's 1835 *Encyclopedia of Gardening* describes both the forcing process and the "blanched and crisp" results as a common "early spring crop in the Netherlands" of long standing.

The forced chicons are sometimes called Belgian endive or French endive. Witloof, however, is the Flemish word for "white leaf" that is used to refer to these delectable morsels in Belgium, by general consent the original home of these buttery, miniature heads. Witloof is offered in most of our seed catalogs, where readers will discover, if they haven't already, a fine confusion about what is endive and what is chicory. If you want to force chicons, be on the outlook for Witloof or Belgian endive or French endive—they are all the same thing. What some catalog copy misleadingly neglects to say is that chicons will not grow by themselves in the garden, but must be forced in the cellar.

A few seed houses offer different strains of Witloof. Le Jardin lists two, VILMORIN 5 and BERGERE. Epicure has carried a Belgian type called ALBA in the past.

Growing and Forcing Witloof

Witloof chicory is sown in the garden in early spring, or even started inside in jiffy pots or flats in early May in colder climates, to be set out in the garden after the frosts are over. The beds where the roots will develop should be very well prepared—double-dug, with plenty of organic material worked in, raked and sifted to fineness, and enriched because the quality of the chicon harvest is determined by the development of the roots. Leaf production should not be stimulated by gathering them for salads, for all the strength of the plant must go into the root. A long growing season and sufficient water gives the root a chance to grow large. If the plants bolt in the summer's heat, cut back the flower stalks, but otherwise leave them undisturbed. The plants may be grown fairly close together if the soil is rich, since heads are not wanted.

In October or November, after the first hard frosts, the heads or leaves are trimmed away to a stub of about 2 inches, and the roots are carefully dug up, with care taken not to injure them. Don't bother to try pulling up the roots by tugging on the chicory heads; the roots are long and go deep into the soil, and will break off more often than they let themselves be pulled up. If you like, of course, you can dig the plants first and cut the tops off afterward.

Any root with a diameter of less than half an inch should be discarded. The roots may be as long as a foot, though the best forcers are in the 6- to 8-inch range—about the size of medium carrots.

The roots are brought into a cool storage resting place that

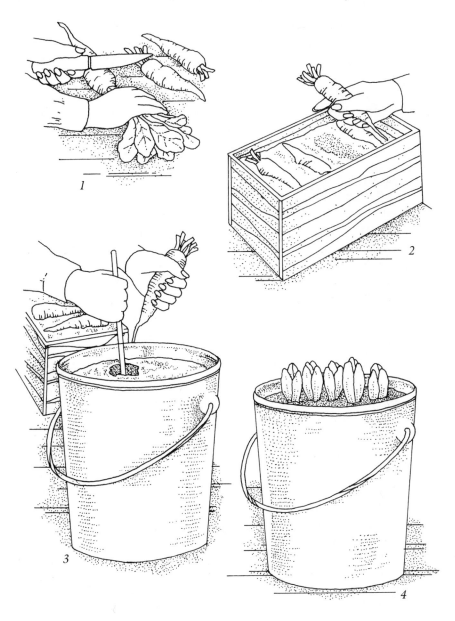

To ensure a good harvest of Witloof chicons, first carefully trim the leaves from the chicory roots to a 2-inch stub (1). Next, place the roots on their sides in a box of sand or peat and set them in cool storage for a month (2). When ready to force, trim each root to a length of 6 to 8 inches; set upright in a box or bucket filled with a mixture of sand and loam (3). Water generously and cover the crowns with 6 inches of dry peat moss or sand (4).

does not freeze up but where the temperature is 32 to 40°F. Here the roots should be stored on their sides in sand or peat for at least a month before starting the forcing process. This rest period deludes the roots into a dormant wintertime mood. When you are ready to start forcing, take only as many roots as you will need, leaving the rest to cool their heels, so to speak. You can stretch the chicon harvest through most of the winter this way.

About a month before you intend to serve your first chicon salad, trim the tips of a number of roots so that they are all about the same length—6 to 8 inches. Set the roots about 2 inches apart in the forcing box, and in an upright position, as if you were planting them.

The forcing box should be about 15 inches deep, with a bottom layer of gravel to aid drainage. Fill the box with a mixture of sand and loam (prepared in the autumn garden and set aside for this very moment), stopping 6 inches below the top. You may use a big plastic bucket or a small barrel or a clean trash can equally well—whatever is at hand that is clean and nontoxic with drainage holes in the bottom.

After the roots are set in place, water them generously, then cover the crowns with 6 inches of dry peat moss or sand. The forcing box is now ready. It must spend its time in complete darkness at a temperature of 50 to 60°F. Higher temperatures will spoil the quality of the chicons. In my local co-op produce market, chicons are offered at stiff prices, but the little heads are loosely furled instead of tight and solid—the sure sign that they were forced at too high a temperature. Some gardeners do not bother covering the roots with the final 6 inches of sand, but instead cover the box with a black plastic bag that has been pierced for adequate air circulation.

In the darkness the chicons will grow until they force their points up through the sand and will be ready for harvest in three to four weeks after they were set in the forcing box. The chicons will be quite brittle and can be snapped off slightly above the crown or cut.

After you've reaped the first harvest, water again, smooth the sand back in place over the crowns, and keep the box in the dark for a second harvest. You may even get a third crop if the roots are strong. The ideal chicon is 5 or 6 inches long, and weighs about 4 ounces.

French Witloof Salad

This salad has a rich, buttery flavor and is delicately bitter. It is the right touch with fresh-caught brook trout if you can arrange to force some chicons during trout season.

6 to 8 chicons, sliced into bite-size pieces
  ½ cup chopped walnuts
  ½ cup watercress, washed, dried, and broken
      into bite-size pieces
  1 small shallot shaved into paper-thin slices
  ⅓ cup olive oil and vinegar dressing

Mix all the ingredients well and let the salad stand 10 minutes at room temperature before serving. All the ingredients should be cool but not chilled.

4 servings

The Green Mixed Salad

This is a robust, well-flavored salad that goes superbly with roasts, chops, or steaks.

  1 head romaine, washed and dried
  1 head blanched chicory or endive, washed and dried
  6 chicons Witloof, cut into bite-size sections
  3 tablespoons rocambole, cut fine
  ½ cup flat-leaf parsley, cut fine
      French or Italian dressing

Tear the romaine and chicory leaves into small pieces and put in a large wooden salad bowl that has been rubbed with garlic. Add the remaining ingredients and mix well. Ten minutes before serving, add the dressing and toss well. The flavors should be blended and the leaves just the slightest bit fatigued, yet still crisp and juicy.

10 to 12 servings

VARIATIONS: Change the character of the salad to a greater delicacy by using larger quantities of the lettuce or by substituting corn salad. Use a blue cheese dressing for a more assertive salad.

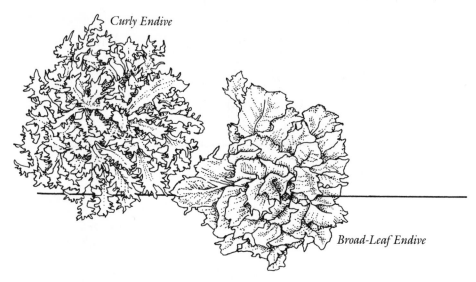

Curly Endive

Broad-Leaf Endive

Endive *(Cichorium endiva)*

Most American gardeners miss the entire endive experience by planting the seeds in late spring, then growing them to maturity in full heat and force of the summer sun. The result is a dark green, tough, very bitter plant which has made thousands into endive haters. But once the gardener has tasted a perfectly grown endive, there is no going back. The endives, tender, young, and blanched, make outstanding salads with character and good texture interest. They cleanse the palate between spicy entrees and add support to a bland main dish like chicken or veal. They add contrast and richness to a lettuce leaf salad and are very good braised or sautéed. The curly types are highly decorative in garnishing buffet dishes. A salad gardener without endives is missing a good thing.

Although both endive and chicory belong to the genus *Cichorium,* the species are different. Endive has as ancient a history as chicory and was well known as a salad vegetable or pot herb to the Egyptians, Greeks, and Romans. It is thought to be of East Indian origin. Ovid makes a reference to the endive in the story of Baucis and Philomen. Certainly by 1548 endive was grown in English gardens, where it was thought to be an aphrodisiac. It was believed that endive should never be pulled up by hand but dug up with a stag's antler on Saint Peter's Day (June 27) or Saint James' Day (July 25). I suspect Saint Peter's

Day endive was more succulent and sweet than one that grew until late July. The early salad green authorities—Gerard, Parkinson, and Evelyn, all described endive as being good for a hot stomach: "cooleth and refresheth the stomacke overmuch heated" and, "It is naturally Cold, profitable for hot Stomachs" are typical praises. Giovanni Baptista Porta's *Natural Magick* gives us many hints on growing and nurturing endives, how to make them sweeter, broader, and whiter:

Endive to grow white
When the leaves are shot forth, you must tie them about the tops with a small string, and cover them over with an earthern vessel set fast into the ground, and the herb will be white . . . our gardeners lay them in sand, and so make them very white.

Sweet Endive
There be many things, which being watered with salt liquors, do forsake their bitternesse, and become sweet. Of which sort Endive is one: and therefore if we would have sweet Endive, *Theophrastus* willeth us, to water it with some salt liquor, or else to set it in some salt places.

One of his best garden hints is a way for "Endive to be tenderer and broader." Endive hearts are still blanched this way in many gardens:

When it is grown up to a pretty bignesse, then lay a small tile-sheard on the middle of it, and the weight of that will cause the endive to spread broader.

Both chicory and endive have about 25,000 seeds to the ounce, and it is a constantly recurring surprise that something so infinitesimal as one of those seeds could produce a fat plant large enough to fill a peck basket.

Endive came early to the New World, and by 1806 Bernard M'Mahon listed three types of endive in *The American Gardener's Calendar*—the "Green Curled," the "White Curled," and the "Broad-Leaved." Today we generally divide endive into two categories. Curly endive has runcinate leaves cut with the lobes facing downward like the dandelion, which give this beautiful plant, perhaps the handsomest of all the salad greens, a frivolous, madcap air. The broad-leaved Batavian endive, also known as escarole, has large, broad leaves whose margins look slightly tweaked and twisted. The curly and broad-leaved endive have many subspecies and strains. J. C. Loudon, in the *Encyclopedia of Gardening,* mentions five varieties in the broad-leaved endive group, and twelve in the curly leaved. In the early nineteenth century, the curly was used for autumn and winter salads, and the broad leaved in soups and stews, and occasionally salads.

Louis Flament of the *Ecole Nationale d'Horticulture de Versailles* included a lengthy section on endives in his little book *Les Salades,* written in the late 1800s.

The French had many varieties to pick and choose among, while the English had only the broad-leaf cultivar BATAVIAN and a curly type known as THE SMALL GREEN. But in France there was the FINE D'ETÉ, which came in the old PARIS strain, and the more modern ANJOU. ROUENAISSE formed a very full rosette and was a good forcer as well as a good plant. FRISÉE DE MEAUX was better grown for winter salads when any greenery was appreciated, for it was not very tender, and the midribs were too large. An endive from Belgium was FRISÉE DE RUFFEC, very resistant to cold and one of the best cultivars for autumn salads. This cultivar is still around. An interesting-sounding sort was C. BÂTARDE DE BOURDEAUX—"The Bastard Chicory of Bordeaux." Flament tells us in *Les Salades* that this was an intermediate type that fell somewhere between the curly endive and the broad-leaved endive and was grown only in the southwest of France where the winters are very mild. Another cultivar best suited to the south of France was VERTE D'HIVER ("winter green").

Only two escarole, or broad-leaf types, are included in his list of desirable cultivars: the VERTE MARAÎCHÈRE or GREEN MARKET, and SCAROLE BLONDE or WHITE ESCAROLE.

Endive is easier to find in seed catalogs than many of the less common salad greens. The most common curly endive offered is apparently the same cultivar under different names— GREEN CURLED or sometimes FRINGED OYSTER or RUFFEC are Louis Flament's Frisee de Ruffec in modern guise. Imagining my salads would have great variety, I once ordered endive seeds under each of these names from different seed houses; there was no visible difference in flavor or growth among them, to my thinking. Green Curled can be ordered from many seedsmen, including Burpee, Park Seed, Vermont Bean Seed, Gurneys,

Twilley, and Herbst Seeds. Another good curly is SALAD KING, which is slow to bolt, quite frost tolerant, and resistant to tipburn. I tested mine (inadvertently) against the frosts and found it brave enough, but rather tough. Park and Herbst both offer it. A Belgian strain of curly is GROSSE POMMANT SEULE (Big Single Head) offered by Le Jardin du Gourmet and Epicure. Jardin has another, WALLONNE, from the Low Countries.

Escarole, or broad-leaved endive, is around in several varieties. Most common is a cultivar called FULL HEART BATAVIAN, which Twilley calls FLORIDA FULL HEART. Herbst Seeds says the strain is different and sells FLORIDA DEEP HEARTED as "deeper and fuller than the Batavian strain." You can get it from Herbst, Twilley, Johnny's Selected Seeds, and Burpee. Epicure offered a Danish strain in a recent year, called NUFEMA. This matures a full ten days earlier than good old Batavian. If it avoids the last minute shift of almost-ready plants from the garden to the cold frame, rejoice. Le Jardin du Gourmet has two cultivars offered by no one else: EN CORNET D'ANJOU and EN CORNET DE BOUR-DEAUX. I tried both of these, but neither did well, largely, I think, because of a hot, dry growing season and repeated absences of the gardener through the summer.

Le Jardin du Gourmet is a particularly good place to order unfamiliar European seed from, for they offer them in small 20-cent packets that allow you to test and sample in small patches and batches before ordering a full-size packet.

William Dam lists two Batavian types. NUMBER 5, which forms large, self-blanching heads in 85 days, and FULLHEART WINTER, both larger and later (95 days) than Number 5. One suspects Fullheart Winter might be closely related to Full Heart Batavian and Florida Deep Hearted.

Suffolk Herbs carries two Italian endives—ENDIVIA RICCIA DI PANCALIERI, a curly type with rose-tinted midribs and a white heart. This should be blanched for several days before harvest to soften the bitterness. The seed can be sown from March to September in mild climates, which will give heads from fall into winter. SCAROLE VERDE A CUORE PIENO is the other, which translates as nothing less than FULL HEART GREEN ESCAROLE! This broad-leaved endive produces an enormous head. The leaves are curled at the outer edges, and the midribs are juicy and tender. The plant is blanched by covering it for several days before harvest. It is, remarks Suffolk, at its best before the summer heat comes on, for it has a tendency to bolt. Most growers start it in an early cold frame and transplant to the garden as early as the weather permits once the plants are in the four-leaf stage.

Growing Endive

Endive is traditionally difficult to bring to crisp, mild-flavored perfection. The seed must be sown either very early so the plants can mature before the midsummer heat, or they must be started in July or August for the heads to finish off in the cool autumn weather. In order to get a mild taste, and an agreeable crispness and creamy color, the heads are blanched as they approach maturity.

Endive likes an ordinary loam, neither greatly enriched nor poor, as well as a consistent supply of moisture. When endives are grown in poor, sandy soils where salad burnet or nasturtium would thrive, the growth is slow and the leaves become tough and bitter. Drought conditions increase the bitterness to the point of inedibility.

For fall endives, plant the seed in the garden in late June or July, or, if your winters are mild, in August. It takes about 90 days for most endives to mature, and they will develop the finest flavors in cool maturation weather. Traditionally, endive is sown following an early lettuce crop, and in the same ground; the soil is perked up a little with a thin layer of compost between the rows or sprinkled over the bed. The seed is sown thinly and covered with a scant one-third inch of mixed sand and humus. Keep the top layer of soil moistened until the seedlings are well up and established. Then they may be thinned to 12 inches apart.

Starting seed directly in the garden in midsummer can be difficult. The soil dries out before the seeds can germinate unless it is kept constantly moist through drip irrigation or a sprinkler. Any mulch heavy enough to conserve moisture smothers the seed and thwarts the emerging seedlings. Most gardeners faced with starting seed in midsummer do it indoors in flats or peat pots, or in a sheltered seedling bed, perhaps in a sunk frame with a shade cloth cover. When the seedlings have four leaves they may be set out on a cloudy day or in the evening and watered copiously.

Once the endives are established, they benefit from mulching that not only holds moisture in the soil, but keeps their roots cool. Endives do not tolerate weeds. It is important to allow plenty of space between the plants, for crowded endives will not make heads.

As the endives mature, after about 65 days of good growing, they are ready to be blanched. In the old days, lengths of fine osier willow were prepared by bending them back and forth in the hands, then splitting them (with the help of a strong fingernail) lengthwise into thin, tough, flexible strips. This free tying material was used to bind up the outer leaves of the endives ready for blanching. Unless you have an osier swamp nearby (alas, I do), tie the outer leaves of the plants up with strips of cheesecloth or soft plant-tying twine. String will cut into the delicate leaves. J. C. Loudon gives us these fine points on blanching in *Encyclopedia of Gardening:*

As the . . . crops advance to full growth, stocky and full in the heart, some should have the leaves tied up every week or fortnight, to blanch or whiten, and to render them tender, crisp, and mild-tasted. Perform this in dry days; and in winter, when the weather is dry without frost. Using strings of fresh bast or small osier twigs, tie the leaves regularly together a little above the middle, moderately close. If the soil be light and dry, earth them up half way; but if moist, merely tie them. . . . The Batavian, from its loftier, looser growth, in every case hearts and blanches better with a bandage. The blanching will be completed sometimes in a week, when the weather is hot and dry; at others, it may take a fortnight or three weeks; after which the endive should be taken up for use, or it will soon rot, in six days or less, especially if much rain fall. To save the trouble of tying, this esculent is also . . . blanched by setting up flat tiles or boards on each side of the plants, which, resting against others in an angular form, and confined with earth, exclude the light. Further, endive may be blanched under garden-pots, or blanching pots. . . . In the heat of summer and autumn, tying up is best; but in wet or cold weather, to cover the plants preserves while it blanches them.

Some gardeners will prefer to blanch following Giovanni Baptista Porta's advice—a broken piece of tile or a slate laid upon the endive head will blanch the heart and broaden the plant.

If drops of rain get down inside the heart of a blanching

endive that is tied up, the results can be disastrous—rotting instead of blanching. Terrified endive growers have been known to open up each plant after a rain, allow the heart to dry out, then tie it up again to continue the blanching process. And, although blanching makes bitter salad greens sweeter, it does slightly reduce the vitamin content. But to most gardeners who see this somewhat arduous process through, the effect of the color gradations from the antique ivory white center through buttery yellow to tenderest lime green to a deep sea green is an extraordinarily beautiful sight.

The game of growing endive becomes most exciting if the first autumn frosts approach before the heads are ready, for frost ruins the delicacies. Gardeners who are determined to enjoy the exquisite endive salads, or who grow endives for the gourmet market, will lift the plants tenderly with a garden fork and transfer them to a waiting cold frame. The frame can be covered with mats to exclude the frost until the heads are finished. The result of such pampering is a very crisp—almost crackling—extremely tender salad of delicate nutlike flavor hinting of hazel and almond—with only a piquant hint of bitterness.

Autumn Salad

A very fine autumn salad of late-season endive is made by mixing a clean, washed head of blanched endive with a handful or more of watercress, chopped celery, and sliced russet or delicious apples. A variation is to substitute slivers of raw turnip for the apple. Chopped hazelnuts, walnuts, or butternuts make a richer, deep-toned salad that goes very well with upland game birds. Many dressings are suited to this combination, from the classic oil and vinegar to a silky cream dressing.

III
Uncommon
Leaves
and Stalks

Knowledgeable gardening and fine salads are inseparable, for the best salads are made of esculent materials and furniture (as John Evelyn called salad greens) freshly picked and cut at the height of perfection, and arranged in the salad bowl within minutes of their plucking, dressed with the finest oils, vinegars and herbs, and brought at once to the table. It is this reward at the table that leads us to seek out more unusual salad greens, to try forcing and blanching techniques, and to search the catalogs eagerly for seeds of coveted varieties. In this chapter are half a dozen plants prized for their leaves or stalks in salads of other countries. Gardeners are conservative, but not as conservative as seed companies, who introduce unfamiliar plants with reluctance. Here are some neglected salad materials that enrich the common lettuces and salad fare in color, flavors, and textures.

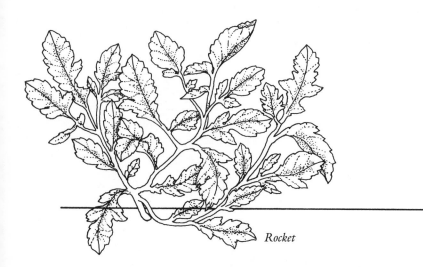

Rocket

Rocket (*Eruca vesicaria* subsp. *sativa*)

Rocket, also called roquette, rugola, rucola, and arugola, seems to be a native of the Mediterranean countries where so many excellent salad greens evolved. The eastern Mediterranean was one of the most heavily traveled corridors in prehistoric migrations, which accounts for the tremendous range of edible plants, including rocket, that grow wild there. Rocket is considered a chic new vegetable in our salad bowls, but it was grown here in colonial days and is on John Winthrop, Jr.'s list of seeds "bought of Robert Hill gr[ocer] dwelling at the three Angells in lumber streete 26th July 1631."

Earlier, John Gerard wrote in his *Herbal* of "sundry kindes of Rocket, some tame, or of the Garden, some wilde, or of the field, some of the water and of the sea." He goes on to say that "Garden rocket, or Rocket gentle . . . hath leaves like those of turneps, but not neere so great nor rough. The stalkes rise up of a cubit, and sometimes two cubits high, weak and brittle; at the top whereof grow the floures of a whitish colour, and sometimes yellowish, which being past, there do succeed long cods, which containe the seed. . . ." He calls it "a good sallet herbe, if it be eaten with Lettuce, Purslane, and such cold herbes." (Most plants were assigned qualities of being hot or cold, dry or moist, and were eaten not only because they tasted good, but because they were good for balanced health if taken in the complicated pre-criptions and quantities that the medical theory of the "Four Cardinal Humours" dictated.) Gerard went on to repeat Pliny's observation on rocket that "whosoever taketh the seed of Rocket before he be whipt, shall be so hardened, that he shall easily endure the paine." Ann Leighton, in her wonderful study *Early American Gardens* (1970), adds to this Nicholas Culpeper's ob-servation in *The Complete Herbal* (1649) that the powers of rocket extend to banishing "the ill scent of the arm-pits." All this and salad too!

Rocket was an important salad green from the time of the ancient Romans through the eighteenth century, but by the nine-teenth century it had lost favor in many gardens, though not in the Mediterranean countries where it still continues to be en-joyed. It was also a good potherb. Giovanni Baptista Porta in *Natural Magick* had some advice for sixteenth century gardeners of rocket and told them how to grow "Sweet Rocket . . . such as will yeeld leaves that shall be more toothsome, if you water it with salt liquor. There is another sleight in husbanding of Pot-herbs, whereby they may be produced fitter to be eaten; and this is by cropping the stalks of them." Cropping the stalks, of course, would force tender new growth, but the saltwater bath is du-bious. What the advice hints is that even the Italians found rocket strong and bitter in taste sometimes. John Evelyn in *Acetaria* includes Spanish rocket in his list of essential salad ingredients and remarks that the young leaves that come immediately after the seedling stage are the best for the salad bowl. That observation is still valid. Rocket must be harvested when young to be good in a salad. A few years ago many seed companies here offered rocket as a smart "new" Italian green, but alas, few gardeners knew how to grow it to best advantage. They seeded it late in spring, then allowed it to grow tall and tough and disagreeable in midsummer as it began to put out flowers. At this point, it had become much too strong in flavor to be edible, and even as a potherb its value is questionable when it gets this old and rank.

But every May I gather tender rocket leaves only 3 or 4 inches tall from under the cloche, add a few early radishes cut paper-thin, and dress this simple salad with pale green cold-pressed Italian olive oil and a few drops of homemade nutty pear vinegar, and serve the aromatic, crisp, delicious result to accompany the orange-fleshed wild brook trout I catch below the garden in the Ompompanoosuc River. It is the most memorable salad of the spring.

Rocket is a half-hardy annual with deeply cut, large wavy leaves that can grow 30 inches tall, or, as John Gerard said, nearly 2 cubits high. *Only the young leaves are good in salads.* Rocket has a rich, faintly spicy taste when young but will develop a disagreeable skunky odor as it matures, which probably accounts for its disappearance from the seed catalogs. When it is grown rapidly in cool weather, it has a piquant, intriguing flavor a little like a hint of horseradish mixed with hazelnuts.

Rocket demands a rich, moist soil and cool growing weather. It should be planted in very early spring when radish seed is sown, and harvested when the leaves are very small, no longer than 6 inches; or, it can be started in late summer for a fall salad crop. Pull the plants before they go to seed unless you want acres of rocket next season.

To harvest rocket, you can either pull the young plants, or cut the leaves, for like many salad greens of the cut-and-come-again nature, rocket will send up successive crops of little green leaves after cutting—what Giovanni Baptista Porta called "croping the stalks." Many growers think the leaves of this second crop are even tastier and more "toothsome" than the first flush.

If rocket is grown in poor, dry soil in the midsummer heat and allowed to flower, it not only tastes and smells unpleasant, but has definite emetic properties. When your rocket plants begin to grow large and the flavor swells from robust to rank, pull them all up and feed them to the hens or the compost heap.

Gertrude B. Foster and Rosemary F. Louden in *Park's Success with Herbs* (1980) suggest following rocket with a planting of dill or summer savory.

Rocket may be mixed with other early greens and lettuces, but the classic use is by itself with finely cut chives and an oil and vinegar dressing, or as a late-season salad containing plenty of ripe, richly flavored tomatoes.

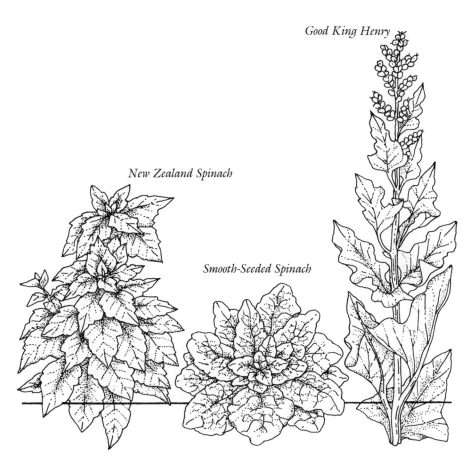

Good King Henry

New Zealand Spinach

Smooth-Seeded Spinach

Spinaches *(Spinacia oleracea)*

The spinaches are annual members of the goosefoot family or Chenopodiaceae, and probably originated in southwest Asia. The goosefoot family has some excellent salad plants as well as the spinaches—beet leaves, which are very good when young in salads, and orach, as well as the wild plant much esteemed by field-salad gatherers of early years, Good King Henry.

Spinach is mentioned as early as the seventh or eighth century in a Chinese work on agriculture, according to one authority, and ancient Arab physicians used spinach in their pharmacopæia. It was apparently first known in Europe in Spain, introduced by the Moors, and for a long time it was known as *olus Hispanicum,* or "the Spanish vegetable," to early botanists. There is a twelfth century reference to it by an enthusiastic Spanish Moor who calls it "the prince of vegetables." *Spinachium* is on a 1351 list of the different vegetables allowed monks on fast days, and 40 years later "spynoches" appear in a cookbook used in the kitchen of Richard II. Spinach was associated with Lent in the late Middle Ages, but it quickly became a favorite vegetable all through the growing season. One spinach story that is probably apocryphal says that Louis XIV (a very great eater) was denied spinach by his doctor and flew into a passion of rage, demanding spinach and remarking witheringly, "What! I am king of France and I cannot eat spinach?"

Most of the early English horticultural writers were lukewarm toward spinach. Gerard wrote, "Spinach is a kind of Blite . . . whose substance is waterie, and almost without taste, and therefore quickly descendeth and looseneth the bellye. It is eaten boiled, but it yeeldeth little or no nourishment at all; it is sometimes windie. . . . It is used in sallades when young and tender. This herbe of all other . . . sallade herbes maketh the greatest diversitie of . . . sallades." Nicholas Culpeper and John Parkinson (in *Paradisi in Sole, Paradisus Terrestris*) see its main use as a salad leaf also, but surprisingly, John Evelyn, the great seventeenth century salad champion, is cool toward spinach. He thought it better cooked than raw, and remarks tartly, "the oftener kept out the better."

We find "1 oz spynadg at 2d" on John Winthrop, Jr.'s list of seeds brought to Massachusetts in 1631 for the colonial garden, and by 1806 Bernard M'Mahon lists three spinach cultivars in *The American Gardener's Calendar.*

There are two types of spinach, one with a rough, single-seeded fruit, known as prickly spinach or winter spinach, and another called smooth-seeded spinach or round-leaved spinach. The so-called prickly seeded spinach is the kind we grow here most commonly, and the smooth seeded is the superb spinach of Italy and other European countries. Waverly Root comments in his magisterial encyclopedia *Food* (1980), "I wonder if the reason for the mediocrity of American spinach is not simply that America plants the wrong seed." Smooth-seeded spinaches, however, are easily purchased from our seed companies once you know which ones they are; only Redwood City Seed informs its customers of the distinction. The Latin name for the smooth-seeded type is *Spinacia oleracea* var. *inermis*. It would be helpful if more seed companies included the Latin name in the catalogs, but only the specialty houses bother.

An old reliable smooth-seeded spinach cultivar known here before 1906 and still popular is BLOOMSDALE LONGSTANDING, an early spinach with thickly wrinkled but tender leaves and very good flavor. There are several strains, including AMERICA and WINTER BLOOMSDALE, the last often sown in fall for an early spring crop in milder climates. An outstanding salad spinach with fleshy tender leaves that hold well into the hot weather is the smooth-seeded Belgian ESTIVATO D'ETE, available from Epicure. It is a delicious spinach. Epicure has another smooth-seed variety, NORES, which I have not grown yet, but it is listed as a long period producer with smooth thick leaves that are very good in salads.

Redwood City offers two less familiar prickly spinaches, MUNSTERLANDER and SOHSHU. Munsterlander is "a very old German strain with arrow-shaped leaves, flat, thin and tender" while Sohshu is a rapid-growing oriental strain that is tolerant to heat. It has smoother leaves than most prickly seeded types. VIRGINIA SAVOY is a very hardy late fall cropping spinach developed at the Virginia Truck Experiment Station in Norfolk to withstand the yellows disease (also called spinach blight) that attacks commercial crops. This spinach will bolt rapidly if planted in spring or summer. Comstock, Ferre & Company carries it. The All-America Winner MELODY HYBRID was bred for home gardeners and is a fast-growing, disease-resistant spinach that's ready in 42 days. It's available from most major seed companies. BENTON NO. 2 is a Japanese hybrid that is fairly tolerant to heat and grows in an upright clump of long-stemmed leaves. HOJO is another Japanese spinach carried by Nichols Garden Nursery and described in its catalog as being "widely grown in the northern provinces of Japan where it is highly prized for its wonderful flavor and good texture." It matures in 45 days and is best planted in late summer for a fall salad. Spinach fanciers will find many other cultivars in the catalogs, including Vesey's 1983 introduction, POPEYE'S CHOICE, a well-flavored, tender spinach reputedly with leaves as large as those of many loose-leaf lettuces, and a good spinach for northern gardens. For salads, it should be harvested when it is 3 or 4 inches high. The different textures and flavors of the spinaches are quite pronounced when they are raw, so you may like to grow a sampler spinach bed to find the sort you like best.

Growing Spinaches

Spinach culture is a little tricky if you are not to have spotty germination and leggy, tough plants. This plant likes a pH of 6.4 to 6.8, and well-manured, well-worked loamy soil in sun or partial shade. It is a cool weather crop that toughens and bolts in dry summer heat. Spinach, like the lettuces and other succulent leaf salad crops, must have adequate water. If denied that vital fluid, it will quickly bolt to seed, under the impression that a killing drought is at hand. Good soil preparation, plenty of water, a weed-free environment and cool weather or artificial shade, make the finest spinaches, too tender when small for mere cooking. These are salad plants.

Spinach is usually sown in earliest spring on through June, every two weeks for steady cropping. As the season's heat intensifies, the salad gardener sows in shadier, cooler beds. It is useful to put up a shade cloth (available from gardening supply establishments) over summer-sown spinach. For the first spinach crop, the bed must be ready to go very soon after the snow and hardest frosts have faded. Young spinach can take light frosts. The best way, is to prepare this bed in the autumn, then mulch it well for winter protection. In early spring, long before the rest of the garden soil can be worked, pull back the mulch and warm the spinach bed soil for a week under a sheet of clear plastic. Sow the spinach thinly, half an inch deep, and cover the seed with cloches or a plastic tunnel if sharp frosts are still expected. After the plants are well up, thin them out to 6 to 8 inches between plants, and use the thinnings in the first salad. Harvest spinach either by picking the outside leaves from the young plants, or by pulling up the entire plant.

A salad spinach bed alternatively may be sown quite thickly, and the young plants thinned out steadily and used in salads as the bed develops.

Fall crop spinach is sown in late summer and protected over winter under cloches or heavy straw mulch or bracken fern mulch. Raised beds are traditional for winter spinach. In early spring the mulch is carefully drawn off the plants, which respond with a very early crop of exceedingly tender, delicious leaves. All the spinaches respond vigorously to rich applications of compost, bone meal, and rotted seaweed.

There are a few plants very similar to spinach in appearance and habit and even taste. These include New Zealand spinach, orach, mustard spinach, and amaranth spinach. All of them are very good in the bloom of youth to add to a green salad for variety and richer color composition.

Borani Esfanaj

Spinach is much used in salads in the Middle East, and a wonderful introduction is Borani Esfanaj.

    1 pound spinach
    1 onion
    1 tablespoon olive oil
    2 cups yogurt, drained
    2 cloves garlic, crushed
    ¼ cup chopped walnuts
       pepper to taste
       mint leaves

Gather and wash the spinach. Place the clean leaves in a covered stainless or enamel pot and mince in the onion. Cook over medium heat for *only 3 minutes* in the water that clings to the leaves.

Drain the semicooked leaves and return them to the pot, adding the olive oil. Put the cover on the kettle but don't return it to the heat. Let the spinach stand for 5 minutes then chill it in the refrigerator.

Strain the yogurt through cheesecloth for 1 hour.

Mix together and chill the yogurt, garlic, walnuts, and pepper. Stir the cold spinach into the yogurt dressing, then heap the creamy salad in a glass bowl, and serve garnished with chopped fresh mint leaves.

4 servings

California Spinach Salad

    4 cups fresh spinach
    1 ripe avocado
    ¼ cup thinly sliced shallots
    2 hard-cooked eggs, peeled
    ½ cup homemade mayonnaise
    4 cups mixed lettuces, washed, dried, and chilled

Put the spinach in a stainless steel bowl or pot and pour boiling water to cover over it. Let it stand 1 minute; then drain at once. (Squeeze the spinach gently to get the water out.)

Chop the spinach, avocado, shallots, and eggs together until the texture is fine but not pureed. The avocado should be peeled and cut into bite-size pieces at the last minute. Mix with mayonnaise in a bowl. Arrange this mixture on the chilled lettuce and serve.

4 servings

VARIATION: Chopped chives or other small onions may be substituted for sliced shallots.

New Zealand Spinach (*Tetragonia expansa*)

This is a half-hardy annual with fleshy, rather brittle leaves, savoyed and rippled. It grows in a mat of triangular leaves and much resembles spinach, but is a slow grower. The plant is a native of New Zealand, where it grew on the edges of the woods in sandy, brushy land. It was discovered by Captain James Cook on his voyage to New Zealand. His crew, starved for green vegetables, cooked the delicious discovery for every meal every day. When New Zealand spinach was first introduced in England in 1772, it was grown as a houseplant for its leaves, but within a few years it was discovered to do very well in the open garden, especially in the heat of summer when spinach bolted. Because New Zealand spinach doesn't bolt in hot and dry weather, it is a good hot weather substitute for spinach. It is grown in place of spinach in hot climates, where it is a favorite leafy green vegetable.

New Zealand spinach is grown much like conventional spinach, but sowing can continue right through the heat of the summer, as long as there is sufficient moisture to keep the plants healthy and growing. You can keep individual plants producing by picking the outer leaves. It goes without saying that the best New Zealand spinach for salads is young, tender, and freshly picked.

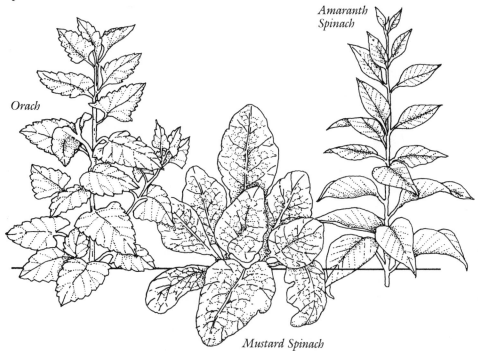

Amaranth Spinach

Orach

Mustard Spinach

Orach *(Atriplex hortensis)*

Also called mountain spinach and butter leaves, this is another ancient annual salad plant much esteemed in earlier days, but now fallen on hard times in our catalogs. It has a mild flavor, and an almost mucilaginous tender texture. The leaves are an unusual pearl gray color when young, similar to the silvery purple green leaves of lamb's-quarters, which is a wild relation. John Winthrop, Jr. included "orradg" in his seed purchase, and Bernard M'Mahon listed three sorts of orach in American gardens in the early part of the nineteenth century—the red, the white, and the dark green. RUBRA, or RED ORACH, is generally available in the herb sections of our seed catalogs. Park Seed, J. L. Hudson, and Nichols Garden Nursery as well as Redwood City Seed all carry orach. It is most often cooked as a potherb, but is good and interesting in salads when it is little. In rich loam, orach will grow a good 6 feet tall, but on poor, sandy soil it keeps a dwarf habit.

Orach can be sown in the bed it will occupy, or started inside for later transplanting, or even grown in pots. It is an easy plant to grow, but to enjoy it in salads, it should be grown rapidly in rich soil with plenty of water and picked when a few inches tall. Although orach plants should be thinned to 2 feet apart when grown for decorative effect or potherbs, you can sow the seed fairly thickly in a salad patch and snip off the plants when they're 3 or 4 inches tall for salads. Mix the leaves with other greens. Early spring and late fall harvests are best.

Mustard Spinach (*Brassica rapa* var. *perviridis*)

This is a quick-growing Japanese green with a spinachy taste. You can sow the seed and gather salads a month later. The small plants (up to 10 inches tall) will stand a lot of heat, but the sturdy cultivar also takes frost on both ends of the season. The leaves are smooth and tender and add interest to the salad bowl. If you make your own salading mixture, or *mesclun* as the French call it, be sure to include the seeds of mustard spinach with a dozen others. Mustard spinach can be bought through Redwood City Seed.

Amaranth Spinach (*Amaranthus tricolor*)

This tall, succulent annual is also called Chinese spinach or Joseph's coat, for its green or red or varicolored leaves. The plant is bushy and vigorous, usually listed with the herbs or ornamental plants in the catalogs. In some places in the world it is a very important summer leafy green vegetable, used in salads and as a potherb, notably in China and India. The stem—tender, soft, and juicy—is sliced and made into salads by itself, or added to leaf salads. In Macao, writes E. Lewis Sturtevant in *Notes on Edible Plants,* it is "the most esteemed of all their summer vegetables." Some strains have red, yellow, and bronze leaves, others a maroon and scarlet leaf that is striking in the salad bowl. J. L. Hudson, Park Seed, Burpee, Redwood City Seed, and Nichols Garden Nursery all carry this beautiful and unusual salad plant. It is an excellent choice for an edible border plant.

Seeds can be sown outside as soon as the danger of frost is

over in a sunny, hot, well-drained bed; or the seed may be started inside and set out. Amaranth spinach also makes good-looking potted plants for on a patio. They are easy to grow, tolerant of soils, but need copious amounts of water in the midsummer. The stems and leaves can be added to salads through the season, though both are best when they are young, with a flavor that has been described as buttered artichoke. This is not one of the huge amaranths but keeps nicely within bounds at about 15 inches when mature. If the plants are allowed to go to seed, they will self-sow. Mark the best plants early in the season with a bit of colored yarn and save them for next year's seed.

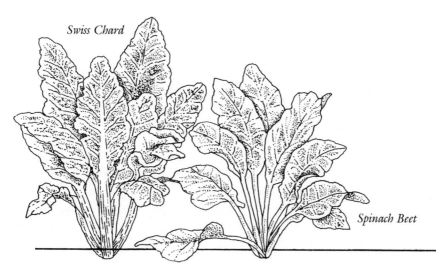

Swiss Chard

Spinach Beet

Swiss Chard and Spinach Beet *(Beta vulgaris* var. *cicla)*

Swiss chard is only one of many beet forms. There are all sorts of beet roots in gorgeous colors from golden yellow to the familiar magenta red of Harvard beets, and the swollen roots are esteemed for everything from borscht to pickles. There are also several excellent foliage beets whose leaves are used like spinach—raw or cooked—and freely added to salads. Swiss chard and spinach beet are two strains of *Beta vulgaris* var. *cicla*. The stems may be cut from the leaves and cooked like asparagus and used in cold salads. The leaves are generally crumpled and savoyed. Swiss chard is listed in many strains in our catalogs, but spinach beet is harder to find—only Thompson and Morgan seem to stock it. The red-stemmed Swiss chard is most common, but the leaves and stems of this handsome plant have a fairly strong, earthy flavor that I, for one, do not find something to write home about in the fresh salad. It is best used quite sparingly, and only when young and mild. Harris Seeds offers a superb white-stemmed Swiss chard that is the best asparagus type that I have tried—it is called LARGE WHITE RIB and makes a good cold cooked salad dish with vinaigrette sauce. When the leaves are very small, perhaps 3 inches tall, stem and leaf can go into salads raw to give a nice meaty but tender texture. LUCULLUS is available from many seedsmen and is our most widely grown Swiss chard, with pale green leaves, and stems that are thick and cream colored.

There are also Swiss chard types with narrow stems and ribs—PERPETUAL is one of these, with a smooth leaf. SWISS CHARD OF GENEVA makes a celerylike bunch of large white stalks, which may be sliced thin and added to a mixed leaf salad for the crunchy, juicy texture, or cooked like asparagus. This is a hardy cultivar.

An unusual European leaf beet is the SILVER-LEAF BEET listed in 1885 in Vilmorin-Andrieux's *The Vegetable Garden* as POIRÉE BLONDE À CARDE BLANCHE. It is a pale, silvery green with broad, short stalks. Epicure carries it as AMPUIS. Add the stalks and leaves to salads for complex textures when the plants are young, but let some mature for the luscious stalks. Cook these and serve them cold on a bed of lettuce with a mayonnaise or cream dressing.

For a very colorful touch, try the Thompson and Morgan Swiss chard mixture with stems in many colors—crimson, yellow, orange, purple, and white.

Celtuce *(Lactuca sativa* var. *angustata)*

This plant is called asparagus lettuce and Chinese stem lettuce. It has been grown in a few gardens here for at least three generations, but only recently have the seed companies picked it up as something new and daring. It has been a favorite vegetable with the Chinese for centuries, and it may have been brought here by some returning traveler or missionary determined not to lose such a fine vegetable.

The pale green leaves are heavy, crisp, and thickly veined, more like robust cos than bibb lettuce. The very young flavorful leaves are best in salads, for once the plants develop size, the leaves become very bitter and tough. It is generally the stem that makes celtuce such a highly esteemed plant. The thick stems can grow up to 5 feet tall, and because they will get woody, they are best harvested when they are less than an inch in diameter. The raw inner cores of the stalks, sliced and added to salads, gives them a crisp texture and subtle, nutlike flavor. The stalks can also be cooked.

Celtuce can be directly sown in the garden, or started inside in flats. It should be seeded as soon as the ground can be worked— preferably earlier, by preparing the bed in the fall and warming its soil for a week with clear plastic in spring before seeding. Celtuce likes a well-worked, enriched soil. Set out the plants or thin them to allow 10 inches between each plant. (Use any thinnings in a salad.) Leaf harvest can start as early as four weeks later, but should end as the leaves start to turn bitter. The stalks will be ready eight to ten weeks after transplanting time. Gather the stalks by cutting them at ground level, and give the leaves to the chickens—if you have a salad garden, a flock of chickens can be raised almost for nothing on the leavings. Peel away the bitter outer stalk until the succulent, tender core remains. Slice these slender rods into the salad or braise them; they are delicate and delicious. Celtuce is offered in almost every seed catalog, but I rarely see it in our gardens.

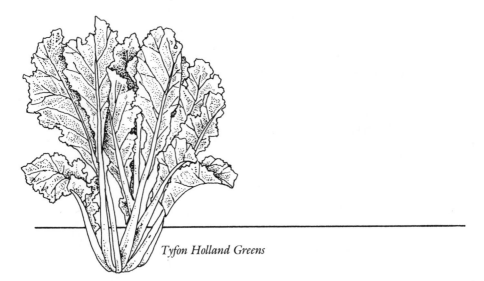

Tyfon Holland Greens

Tyfon Holland Greens

This is a new listing of Nichols Garden Nursery in Oregon, and at the time of writing this seems to be the only seed house carrying it. It is a member of the Cruciferae family and is a new cross between stubble turnips and Chinese cabbage. It has a mild, agreeable flavor and is used, according to the Nichols, in salads, in stir-fried oriental dishes, and as a potherb. The plant is hardy and does well as a cut-and-come-again salad plant. It does not suffer from the "mustardy" flavor you might think a derivative from a turnip would have. Cut it for salads when it is 4 or 5 inches high, but if some plants grow out-of-bounds, feed them to the chickens or stock. These greens are grown locally in Oregon as stock forage, but it's a fine addition to our salad bowl.

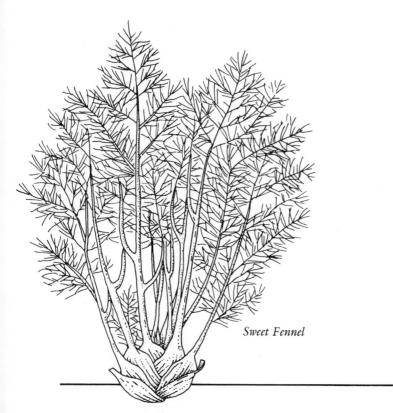

Sweet Fennel

Fennel *(Foeniculum vulgare)*

Fennel is not usually thought of as a salad plant, nor are the mints, but both are very pleasing to the palate in a salad. The fennels are very old plants, apparently native to the Mediterranean countries, and they have many virtues from kitchens to medicine chest. The Romans used fennel for everything—meats, salads, sauces, dainties. Charlemagne, in later days, took a personal interest in fennel and commanded it be grown on every one of the Imperial farms. The major types spread through Europe over the centuries until Gerard could write that fennel was too well known to need a description. Fennel was good for the eyesight, helped nursing mothers make milk, perked up the kidneys, lungs and liver, and curbed stomach wambles and flatulence. John Parkinson lists three fennels, two of them sweet. Pickles and fish were improved by fennel, he wrote, and the seeds went into breads and pies to improve the flavors by a faint and mysterious aromatic. Other authors expanded the powers of fennel to embrace a preventive strength against jaundice, gall stones, and gout as well as snakebite and herb poisoning.

Two of the fennels came to America with John Winthrop, Jr.—on his list of seeds he indicated "1 oz fennell seed" and "½ oz sweet fennel"—and Bernard M'Mahon listed it in the early nineteenth century. Yet modern American gardeners have forgotten how excellent the fennels can be.

Foeniculum vulgare is an herb grown for its flavorful leaves and seeds. For centuries it has been used, as Parkinson described, "to trimme up and strowe upon fish." In France, the stalks of this herb fennel are dried and tied up in bundles that make an aromatic smoke when tossed onto the small open fire considered correct for grilling sea bass. There is also a decorative bronze fennel, very attractive for borders. Sir Winston Churchill grew fennel in order to raise swallowtail butterflies, which, in the caterpillar stage, fed on the foliage and stems.

Another fennel is a famous regional delicacy—carosella (*Foeniculum vulgare* var. *azoricum*), also called Sicilian fennel. This is a warm climate plant with pencil-size juicy stems that are cut up into salads or eaten whole. At the end of the nineteenth century, Sturtevant's *Notes on Edible Plants* describes it as

> The famous *carosella,* so extensively used in Naples, scarcely known in any other place . . . used while in the state of running to bloom; the stems, fresh and tender, are broken and served raw, still enclosed in the expanded leaf-stalks.

This fennel seems to be available only to Italian gardeners, and a diligent search of the seed catalogs fails to turn it up.

The third fennel, *Foeniculum vulgare* var. *dulce,* or sweet fennel, is also called Florence fennel or finocchio. The stalks enlarge into very thick, meaty spoons at their bases which overlap one another to resemble a swollen bulb. The mild, sweet anise flavor and succulent crispness adds piquancy to salads. Californians know and enjoy this delicious vegetable (which can be cooked and prepared in scores of ways), but it remains mysterious to many gardening salad lovers. Nearly every seed company offers it, so include a few plants in your salad garden if you have not yet had the pleasure. Cut the raw stalks into mixed salads, or make an unusual but simply dressed fish accompaniment with paper-thin fennel slices that have soaked for an hour in ice water with a crushed clove of garlic.

It was once believed in England that snakes ate fennel before shedding their skins, for it was a tonic that rejuvenated them and improved their eyesight. It was often hung over doorways for its antiwitch properties, yet people tried to find it growing wild rather than plant it in the garden in belief of an old verse, "Sow fennel, sow trouble."

Fennel likes cool weather and a dampish climate. I grew some wonderful fennel years ago when I lived in Vermont's Northeast Kingdom near the Canadian border, during a chilly summer of endless drizzle.

Start the seed early in the garden or inside in flats. The soil should be only slightly acid. Thin the plants to stand 8 inches apart, and keep the fennel bed free of weeds and liberally watered during dry spells. Fennel responds wonderfully to drip irrigation. As the basal club begins to swell to the size of an egg, heap soil up around it. The blanching will make the anise flavor subtle and fine. If you do not blanch, the vegetable will taste as strong as a licorice stick. Harvest the fennel when the bulbs are a few inches in diameter and still tender.

Fennel Slaw

Grate coarsely or finely shred 1 fennel bulb in a chilled bowl and toss thoroughly with a vinaigrette dressing. Slivers of radish may be added for a variation. One bulb will grate enough for 2 servings.

Finocchio Salad

Use salad tomatoes, cultivars with meaty walls and little pulp, to prevent a pinkish puddle of tomato juice in the bottom of the bowl.

          3 cups tender mixed leaf lettuces
          2 cloves garlic
          3 cups fennel, cut into matchsticks
          2 thoroughly ripe salad tomatoes
    ½ to ⅔ cup Italian dressing

Wash, spin-dry, and chill the lettuce.

Smash the garlic enough to release its fragrance; then put it in a large bowl of ice water. Add the fennel to the ice water and chill for 1 hour.

Shortly before the salad is to be served, drain and dry the fennel. Arrange the lettuce on a deep platter. Heap the fennel in the center; then slice and arrange the tomatoes around the fennel. Pour the dressing over the salad and serve.

6 servings

VARIATION: Substitute 2 heads butterhead lettuce for leaf lettuces.

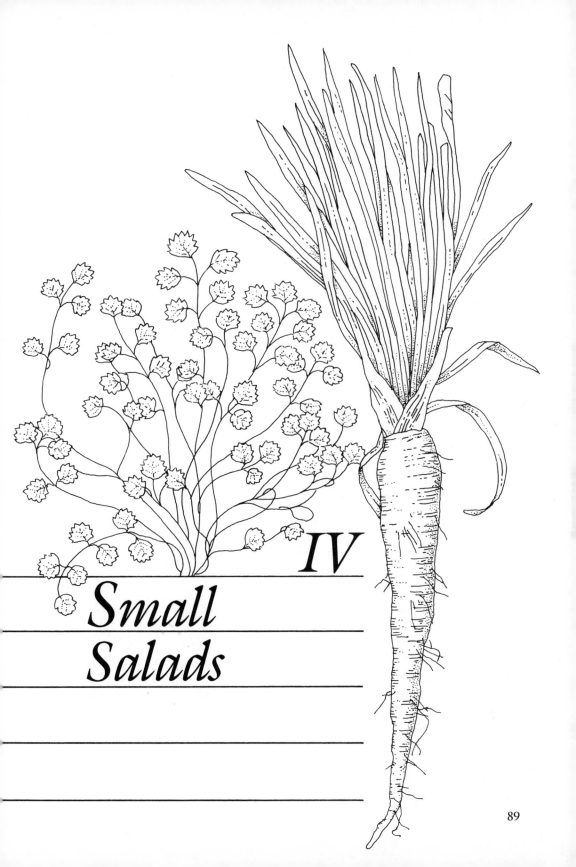

IV
Small Salads

E ven a hundred years ago "small salads" was the phrase for the lesser herbs and diminuitive greens that were usually mixed with the lettuces, chicories, and endives. These small salads included the low-growing, juicy purslane, the garden cresses and water cress, corn salad and burnets, radish leaves, mustard greens, and dozens of wild salad fodder plants. Most of these low-growing, well-flavored plants are still grown in European salad gardens, but here very few gardeners bother with them any more, partly because the plants have slipped from modern attention and partly because they are hard to find in our more common seed catalogs, although specialty seed houses offer most of them after a little searching. The salad fancier will be delighted with the rich range of leaf and color that add so much to a salad. These small salad plants deserve a little corner of the garden and repay the space with taste sensations and visual pleasures that are simply not available at the produce counter; if you want these plants, you must grow them.

Early salads were much more diverse than our modern leaf conglomerations. The Roman Columella gave variations on a basic salad recipe of "savory, mint, rue, coriander, parsley, chives or green onion, lettuce leaves, colewort, thyme or catmint and green flea-bane." (Some of the edible artemisias were also used to drive fleas from clothing in less fastidious times.) Bridget Henisch's *Fast and Feast* lists several wonderfully rich gatherings of salad furnishings that most gardeners today would find difficult to duplicate:

> One very pretty salad was made from violet petals, onions and lettuce, while a fifteenth-century list of herbs 'for a salade' includes parsley, mint, cress, primrose buds, daisies, dandelions, rocket, red nettles, borage flowers, red fennel, and chickweed.

A century earlier than this, what must have been a rather high-flavored salad was dressed with oil and vinegar and included parsley, sage, garlic, onions, leeks, borage, mint, fennel, cress, rue, and rosemary all in the same bowl. Flowers were much used in salads, and included violets, roses, hawthorn, primrose, and carnations.

The green salads of the past held no such rude intruders as sliced tomatoes and radishes and cucumbers and green peppers and celery. Andre Simon, writing for the Wine and Food Society of London, wrote acerbically on the subject:

> . . . Green salads . . . are really best served by themselves, with a dressing of olive oil, wine vinegar or lemon juice . . . ; salt and pepper, and neither sugar nor mustard, but some finely-chopped mixed herbs, such as parsley, chervil, tarragon, chives, and, if liked, a mere suspicion of garlic. Radishes, tomatoes, cucumber and the like are very often added to green salads, in England and the U.S.A., but their inclusion in the green salad bowl is sheer heresy: they are much better served separately, as hors d'oeuvres. . . .

Readers who think that the great food authority was talking through his hat must first try a true green salad mixed his way and include a rich selection of the varied salad leaves in season; this is indeed a noble salad.

There are some very worthy small salad plants that deserve to come out of obscurity and into our gardens again. Enjoy growing these unusual salad leafages and mixing them in with the lettuce and endive and chicory. Experiment in changing the whole character of your salads with a handful of different raw materials—the juicy fleshy stems and leaves of purslane, the nip of the cresses, the flash and dash of nasturtium flowers, the cooling freshness of mint and burnet, the rich bitterness of endive, the crackling of fresh fennel stalks sliced thin. Try for the exciting and full mixtures of dozens of plants in your salads instead of the same old, tiresome and soggy lettuce, tomato and cucumber, which make a heavy, wet salad instead of the light glistening mass of greens that cleanses the palate between courses and enhances everything from roast beef to sweet and sour pork.

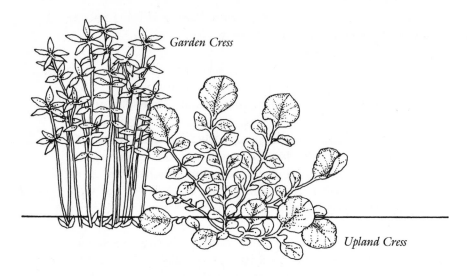

Garden Cress

Upland Cress

Cresses (*Lepidium* spp.)

There are hundreds of cresses, most wild, many domesticated, and nearly all eaten in some part or other of the world, though only a few cultivars are generally available to gardeners in North America. A large genus of edible cresses are the *Lepidium* group. E. Lewis Sturtevant mentions, among many, *L. draba*, the hoary cress of the eastern Mediterranean, and *L. latifolium*, better known as dittander, or poor man's pepper, once much grown in English cottage gardens as an excellent salad plant. Even today the cresses are keenly enjoyed in the English salad, especially in the winter salad mixture known as mustard and cress, a blend of *L. sativum* and *Sinapsis alba*.

The most common cresses in the garden are those grouped under *Lepidium sativum*. Sturtevant divides this large group into four basic types, although there are at least a hundred different cresses known. They are: common cress, curled cress, broad-leaved cress, golden cress. He lists 37 synonyms for these cresses, for they are among the oldest salad plants known and apparently came to the Mediterranean from the Near East. The Greeks and Romans grew domestic cresses in their gardens, and by the late Middle Ages John Gerard wrote the following in *Herbal*:

Galen saith that the cresses may be eaten with bread . . . and so the ancient Spartans usually did; and the low countrie men many times doe, who commonly use to feed of Cresses with bread and butter. It is eaten with other sallade herbes, as Tarragon and Rocket; and for this cause it is chiefly sown.

The very commonness of the cresses gave rise to a saying—"not worth a cress," which has been corrupted over the centuries to "not worth a curse."

Lepidium sativum, or garden cress, is a bright green, very attractive, rapidly growing small-leaved plant that can be enjoyed in salads only two or three weeks after the seed is sown. J. C. Loudon remarked in *Encyclopedia of Gardening*, "It ranks among gardeners as the principal of the small salads." He lists six cresses, adding to Sturtevant's basic four, the "Normandy Curled Cress, . . . forming a beautiful garnish throughout the winter, preferred by Mr. M'Intosh, a first-rate gardener, to every other cress . . ." and the "Broad-Leaved Normandy."

Growing Cresses

Garden cress is often grown in winter in windowsill gardens, and has been a quick-sprout novelty for generations of school children who sprout it on damp blotting paper. Sometimes it is offered in seed form along with a ceramic head or woolly animal that obligingly sprouts "hair" or "wool," the dense green growth of the cress leaves. In the nineteenth century, cress was grown seriously in cone-shaped earthenware pots with gutters on the sides to hold the dampened seeds. These objects were called cress cones.

Garden cress is a very early plant that enjoys a cool growing season, and it can get bitter and hot as it ages. Cress fanciers sow the seed every three weeks or so for a continuous supply. As the summer peaks, cress can be grown in a shady place or even shaded by a cloth. This is an easy plant to find in most seed catalogs.

It is fairly simple to grow cress (and mustard) inside in the winter. Use a flat filled with peat or sterilized soil (damping off can be troublesome if just garden earth straight from the plot is used), or even a folded piece of wetted burlap. Sow the seed evenly and thickly. Do not cover the seeds with soil, but just cover the flat with a sheet of glass to keep the moisture in until the seeds germinate. Remove the glass, and water the cress when it needs it with cool but not cold water. Cut them for the salad when they are 2 or 3 inches tall. Cress takes longer to grow than mustard by a few days, so sow the mustard seed three or four days after the cress.

Twice as much cress as mustard should be used in the salad bowl, and a classic treatment of these bright little plants is to mix together in a salad bowl two parts cress, one part mustard, and a few spoonfuls of finely chopped apple, the whole dressed with oil and vinegar and decorated with rose or nasturtium petals.

Thomas and Betty Powell in *The Avant Gardener* (1975) wrote that "Vegetable growers are growing more salad plants than ever before. The cresses especially are desired." They list two garden cresses as a substitute for watercress, our friend *Lepidium sativum* and *Barbarea vulgaris*, for which they give the common name, upland cress. (It is also known as winter cress and Saint Barbara's herb.) They add, "Upland cress tastes most like watercress, while peppergrass is somewhat 'hotter.' " Today upland cress is usually listed in seed catalogs as *Barbarea verna*, and there are few references to *L. sativum* as peppergrass.

Barbarea verna is very old. It came early to this country and now grows wild everywhere from Canada to Missouri, an escapee from Colonial gardens. The wild form looks much like the wild mustards with similar little yellow flowers, but beneath its major leaves *B. verna* has small basal leaves like tiny green ears. Ann Leighton, in *Early American Gardens*, quotes John Gerard as saying "Herbe Saint Barbara" belonged among the salad herbs "equall with Cresses of the Garden, or Rocket." Cress, of course, was on John Winthrop, Jr.'s seed list, but whether *B. verna*, or *Lepidium sativum* or *Nasturtium officinale* no one knows. It is interesting to note that Peter Henderson, one of our major nineteenth century garden writers, mentions in his still-useful book, *Gardening for Pleasure* (1895), a cultivated cress that may be a domestic strain of *B. verna*. "There is," he writes, "a variety recently introduced known as 'Upland Cress,' that can be grown in an ordinary garden. It is almost identical in flavor with the Water Cress."

Barbarea verna was called Saint Barbara's herb because it was the only edible green plant around on Saint Barbara's Day (December fourth), according to Euell Gibbons, who was a keen fancier of this cress and wrote one of his most famous diatribes in its defense in *Stalking the Wild Asparagus* (1962). He angrily described the smug Philadelphia suburbanites driving past the Italian women gathering *B. verna* early in the spring from the wild:

There's nothing smart about eating poor food and getting gypped in the bargain, when nature is offering so much better fare for the taking. If I followed one of those buxom Italian women home, I'll bet I would get a much better dinner than I would if I had to eat the force-grown, sprayed, processed, refrigerated, devitalized products for which the suburban housewife thought it smart to pay good money.

Upland cress prefers rich, moist ground and is a hardy biennial that can be mulched overwinter in cold climates. If you can get under the mulch during the winter, the tasty leaves are there for salad. Upland cress grows thick clusters of bright green leaves in the early spring, as soon as the snow is gone and before any other salad plant appears. It is faintly aromatic and somewhat nippy in taste. The leaves must be plucked while the weather is still cold, for the plant becomes disagreeably bitter as soon as the frosts are past. Start the seed in the garden in late summer, and thin it to 4 to 6 inches between plants. Mulch as the winter comes on, and the next spring while the smart suburbanites are buying limp lettuce in the supermarket, you will be enjoying a crackling fresh helping of upland cress salad.

Redwood City Seed offers LAND CRESS or *Barbarea praecox*, while J. L. Hudson has *Barbarea verna*. Mustard-and-cress seed may be ordered from The Urban Farmer.

Salad maniacs on the lookout for novelties might want to watch along with me for something called Thracian cress in Andre Simon's *Vegetables* in *A Concise Encyclopedia of Gastronomy* (1941, 1948). He says:

> A comparatively new kind of Cress in England, but one that is widely distributed in the Balkans. . . . it is . . . well deserving the attention of gastronomes, particularly those who have a garden; it combines the mustard-oil flavour of mustard (in the mustard-and-cress seedlings) with that of raw cabbage, and it is a valuable addition to many green salads and to practically any vegetable salad, particularly potato salads, haricot salads and others.

Mustard and Cress Salad in Early Autumn

Always use twice as much cress as mustard. Wash, shake dry, and toss the mustard and cress into a salad bowl. Chop a well-flavored apple—a russet, Empire or Liberty—and add it to the bowl. Add a light olive oil and pear vinegar dressing, toss the salad well and scatter nasturtium petals over all. Serve at once.

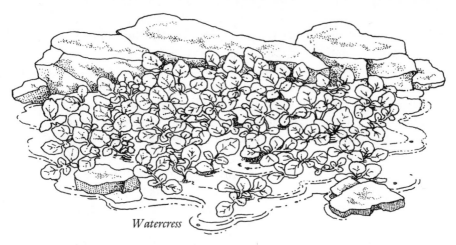

Watercress

Watercress (*Nasturtium officinale*)

The peppery, crisp leaves of the familiar (and expensive) watercress are used in salads, sandwiches, soups, and to dress up prime ribs and chops. This is one of the oldest plants known to man, and, according to Pliny the Elder, watercress was considered a brain stimulant. A Greek proverb went "eat cress and gain more wit." Would that it were more widely grown today! Watercress has been used not only to sharpen mental acuity, but as an antiscorbutic since ancient days. The Romans, on their sweep through Europe, introduced it everywhere. It was much cultivated in the Middle Ages as the basic ingredient in a salve thought to be particularly effective with sword wounds.

Growing Watercress

Watercress is a perennial aquatic plant of the north temperate regions. J. C. Loudon's description of its culture in *Encyclopedia of Gardening* still has much information of interest:

The most suitable description of water is a clear stream, and not more than an inch and a half deep, running over sand or gravel; the least favorable, deep still water on a muddy bottom. It is highly advantageous to make the plantations in newly risen spring-water, as the plants not only thrive better in it, but, in consequence of it being rarely frozen, they generally continue in vegetation, and in a good state for gathering through the whole winter season. The plants are disposed in rows parallel with the course of the stream. In shallow water, the distance between the rows is not more than eighteen inches, but in deep water it is as much as from five to seven feet. When the plants begin to grow in water one inch and a half deep, they soon check the current so as to raise the water to the height of three inches about the plants, which is considered the most favorable circumstance in which they can be placed. Where the plants are not in rows, the water is impeded in its course, and the plants are choked up with weeds and the different matters which float down the stream; and when the cress is grown in deep water, the roots are easily drawn out of the soil in gathering. The cress will not grow freely in a muddy bottom, nor will it taste well. . . .

Watercress should be planted along the margins of pools fed with fresh water, or along quiet-flowing, small streams. I cannot do much with watercress in Vermont, for as the snow melts and runs off, even the tiniest rivulet becomes a raging torrent choked with ice and branches that scour away the unfortunate watercress. Very small streams dry up in the summer. Best is a spring-fed pool or a very wet place through which water runs, or a contained cress bed near the garden water tap. Stagnant water or shade are both poor environs for watercress. The plant may grow entirely submerged, or may thrust its leaves above the water. Once it gets going, it can choke out all other growth in a pool.

Watercress must have a cool climate, sunlight, and very clean running water to be at its best. Some seed suppliers advise gardeners to grow cress in the shade, but this is a mistake. Watercress needs sunlight.

Water pollution is very widespread these days, and much of the watercress discovered growing "wild" may be contaminated by sewage or other pollutants. Have your water source tested before sowing cress seed. Another problem for cress lovers is the increasing acidity of our streams. Watercress likes and does best in streams that meander through limestone, and it grows marvelously well in Britain's chalk streams.

Watercress seed, available from many seedsmen, may be started indoors in pots of moist soil. The temperature should be around 55°F, and the seeds should not be covered over. The soil must be kept very moist. When the small plants are well rooted, they can be transplanted to the sunny, clean-water-fed pool or brooklet. Watercress will also root easily from cuttings inserted in wet sand.

Some gardeners have had success starting watercress inside around early March (in Connecticut) and then transplanting it to a small hotbed a month later. The modern hotbed is more likely to be heated by a heat cable than buried horse manure or hot water pipes of yore. The plants are set 8 inches apart and the soil kept very wet. The earliest watercress can be harvested about five weeks after the young plants were set out, and they will produce a crop up until June. The same trick can be applied at the end of the season by starting the seed in mid-August and setting it in the hotbed around September 15 for a late October crop.

A cold frame and a drip irrigation emitter positioned in the right place also works. Watercress is at its prime early in the season before it flowers, for the leaves become smaller, tougher, and rather bitter as the season goes on.

Another aquatic cress often mentioned in the older gardening literature is *Veronica beccabunga*, known better as brooklime or water pimpernel, native to the British Isles and very hard to find elsewhere. This was a favorite salad green in Scotland, and bunches of the sprigs were brought to market under the name of water-purpy. J. C. Loudon describes it: "The young tops and leaves are used as a salad, like the water-cress, with which it is often mixed, being milder, more succulent, and only slightly bitterish in taste." Gardeners may come across brooklime in travels through England and Scotland.

Watercress Salad

This is the simplest of salads, and it is excellent with cold roast beef, a grilled chop, planked swordfish, or even ham and eggs.

>   2 cups watercress
>   olive oil and lemon juice dressing

Rinse well, dry, and chill the watercress. Toss the watercress in a chilled bowl with an olive oil and lemon juice dressing. Season to taste with freshly ground pepper and serve.

4 servings

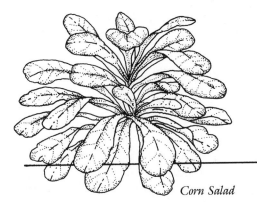

Corn Salad

Corn Salad (*Valerianella locusta* var. *olitoria*)

This excellent salad plant is also known as lamb's lettuce, *mâche*, fetticus, and feldsalat, depending where you come from. That prickly reformer, William Cobbett, was one of the most vociferous champions of the cottage garden and the depressed agricultural worker in the early nineteenth century, but he had a maddening way of dismissing what did not please him with a few short, scornful words, and very few of the small salad plants pleased him. Of corn salad he said in *Cottage Economy*:

> This is a little, insignificant annual plant that some persons use in salads, though it can hardly be of any real use, where lettuce seed is to be had. It is a mere *weed*.

Millions of salad lovers know better, particularly in France where *mâche* is greatly esteemed for its delicate amelioration of the more sharply flavored salad greens. The subtle flavors and good leaf of the corn salads are highly prized by salad connoisseurs. Moreover, corn salad can be picked long before the earliest lettuces are ready. The classic French way of serving *mâche* is with thin slices of cold cooked beets and raw celery and a vinaigrette dressing made with lemon juice instead of vinegar. John Evelyn in *Acetaria* remarked that "Corn-sallet" was ". . . loos'ning and refreshing: the Tops and Leaves are a *Sallet* of themselves, seasonably eaten with other Salleting, the whole Winter long, and early Spring: the French call them *Salad de Preter*, for their being generally eaten in *Lent*."

Corn salad was gathered in the wild long before domesticated cultivars came into the garden. John Gerard mentions in the *Herbal* that corn salad was becoming popular in England and "hath been sowen in gardens as a sallad herbe." John Winthrop, Jr. had it on his long seed list, and Bernard M'Mahon listed it in 1806 in his *Gardener's Calendar*. Obviously corn salad was grown more often in the salad gardens of two hundred years ago than it is today.

The English garden writer, Joy Larkcom, in a survey of Belgian vegetables for the Royal Horticultural Society's journal, *The Garden*, remarks on the popularity of corn salad in Belgium. "A quarter of Gonthier's customers order it—and they have eight varieties to choose from, varying in colour and shape of leaf, hardiness and 'heartiness'." Corn salad is increasingly listed in our seed catalogs, most often simply as "corn salad," usually a strain imported from Holland with large, round leaves. Epicure has the French cultivar A GROSSE GRAINE, a dark green, compact *mâche*, as well as CAVALLO, described as a German feldsalat. Le Jardin du Gourmet carries several corn salad cultivars, including A Grosse Graine, VERTES D'ETAMPES, VERTE DE CAMBRAI, and RONDE MARAÎCHÈRE. The Urban Farmer offers no less than six corn salad cultivars—GROTE NOORDHOLLANDSE MACHOLONG from the Netherlands: Ronde maraichere; a German strain of VERTE DE CAMBRAI; another German type—DUNKELGRÜNER VOLLHERZIGER (or, "The Full-hearted Dark Green Fieldsalad"); the French ETAMPES, still popular after a century in the gardens of Europe; and a large-leaved English variety called simply ENGLISH corn salad. The Urban Farmer also offers a nice corn salad sampler combining all six of their corn salads. I have not yet seen the Italian corn salad (VALERIANELLA ERIOCARPA) which has spoon-shaped, slightly hairy leaves about 5 inches long, listed in any of our catalogs. It is reputed to do well in warm climates and to have an even milder flavor than the cool-climate types.

Growing Corn Salad

The corn salads are small, annual plants that are quite frost tolerant. They make a cool-weather crop, like so much of the best salad greenery. The seed is often sown late in the summer for a late autumn crop in mild climates. More often it is sown in late fall for an early spring salad. If seed is sown in late summer in cold climates it can be mulched overwinter with some success. Northern gardeners may also start it inside very early and transplant it to a cold frame outside for an early summer crop.

Corn salad prefers a very rich soil with plenty of manure and compost worked in. Joy Larkcom comments that it is a good candidate for intercropping in the onion bed, sown a little before the onions are harvested. Corn salad needs plenty of moisture and benefits from mulching. It can be harvested as a rosette head in 45 to 60 days, or, the small tender leaves can be picked from the time they are beyond the seedling stage. Some fanciers sow a thick bed of corn salad and cut the plants at ground level. Others like to blanch their corn salad heads as they mature for the buttery flavor and the pale green effect in the salad bowl.

The Urban Farmer owners are lovers of corn salad and eat it fresh from the garden year-round. Their remarks in a recent catalog on winter harvesting are useful if you grow late-season plants in the open garden:

The Corn Salad, Tendergreen and Mizuna are most special because they provide a fresh green salad. Harvesting must be done when there is no snow cover and the temperature is at or near freezing on the ground where the plants are growing (the air temperature one foot off the ground may be much colder). If there is a snow cover the plants will be bruised in brushing it away. When the temperature is too cold the plants will be wilted and easily bruised. Thus, early afternoon on a sunny day is the time to harvest.

If you have a few cloches, try setting them over corn salad plants as the winter weather comes on. They make harvesting salads in winter a good deal more convenient.

Dry, sandy soil is a very poor place to start corn salad seeds, and germination rates will be low. Once your young plants are up, watch out—all animals, from woodchucks to chickens, adore corn salad in any stage of development more than any other vegetable. A corn salad patch has to be protected where the deer and the antelope play, or there will be no harvest.

Salade Lorette

This is the classic salad made with *mâche*.

1 pound young leaves of *mâche*
2 cups cooked, drained beets, sliced thinly
1 stalk celery, sliced into matchsticks or julienned
  French dressing

Wash, spin-dry, and chill the *mâche*. Mix the ingredients and the dressing quickly and serve at once.

4 servings

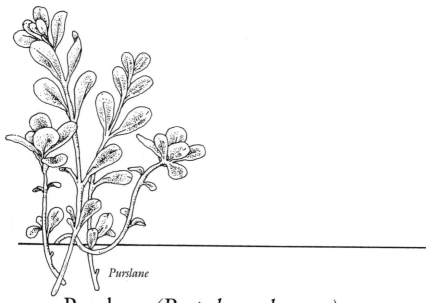

Purslane

Purslane *(Portulaca oleracea)*

Purslane is another ancient salad plant whose Sanskrit name has left traces in many languages. Theophrastus and Columella both praised it to the skies, and today it is still a very fine salad plant much used all over the world except here. With us, unfortunately, the wild form of "pusley" is so feared and despised for its rampant, spreading habit, that most gardeners pale at the thought of deliberately introducing to their gardens any plant that is related to such a bad actor. Wrote Charles Dudley Warner in his delightful *My Summer in a Garden* (1871), "ambitious 'pusley,' which grows with all the confidence of youth and the skill of old age. It beats the serpent as an emblem of immortality." William Cobbett, of course, outdid himself in spleenishness by calling it "a mischievous weed that Frenchmen and pigs eat when they can get nothing else. Both use it in salad, that is to say, raw."

But all the early garden and herb treatises praise the "great purslane" (as opposed to the small, wild purslane) as a fine salad green. John Gerard is almost rhapsodic in his description of the domestic purslane as having "stalkes . . . round, thick, somewhat red, full of juice, smooth, glittering, and parted into certaine branches trailing upon the ground, the leaves be an inch long, somewhat broad, fat, glib . . ." and makes a clear distinction between this fine plant and its lesser relative, which "cometh up of his own accord in allies of gardens and vineyards."

In 1619 Samuel de Champlain, coming from purslane-loving France to the New World, noted his puzzlement in *Les Voyages* at the attitude of the Indians on the Maine coast toward purslane "which grows in large quantities among the Indian corn, and of which they make no more account of than weeds." Familiarity breeds contempt.

The French cultivated variety of purslane has large, fleshy, golden leaves that have a slightly acid savor and a juicy, gelatinous texture. It is milder than the wild green sort, very rich in iron, vitamins A and C, and can elevate a salad from the pedestrian to the exotic. This golden purslane earned high salad marks from John Evelyn who wrote of it as

> . . . being eminently moist and cooling, quickens Appetite, asswages Thirst, and is very profitable for hot and *Bilious* tempers, as well as *Sanguine*, and generally entertain'd in all our *Sallets*, mingled with the hotter herbs. . . .

Growing Purslane

Purslane likes a rich, well-drained soil in full sun. The seed can be sown in late spring when danger of frost is past. In Belgium, purslane is often sown under cloches or in frames in April and uncovered when frost damage is unlikely. The plants are mature in about 60 days, and the leaves should be picked off the ends of the newest shoots, leaving two or three at the base for continuous growth. The leaves ought to be harvested before the flowers appear for the finest quality.

If you are afraid your garden will be taken over by purslane, do not allow the plants to set seed and remove all parts of the plant at the end of the season. Never, never rototill purslane into the garden, for each stem joint can root. The moisture stored in purslane's stems means the seed can mature even after the plant is pulled up. I toss my unwanted purslane into the chicken yard where it is greatly appreciated, and where not a shred goes un-eaten. Some ultracautious gardeners never let salad purslane into their gardens but grow it in large pots.

The seed of the FRENCH GOLDEN LEAVED PURSLANE can be gotten from Le Jardin du Gourmet (where it is listed as POUR-PIER) and from William Dam.

Sorrel

Sorrel (*Rumex* spp.)

John Evelyn says only the fine young leaves of sorrel with the first shoots are to be used in the salad bowl and lists several favorite cultivars grown in seventeenth century gardens:

> The French *Acetocella*, with the round Leaf, growing plentifully in *North* of *England*; *Roman Oxalis*; the broad *German*, &c. but the best is of *Green-Land*; by nature cold, Abstersive, Acid, Sharpening Appetite, asswages Heat, cools the Liver, strengthens the Heart; is an *Antiscorbutic*, resisting Putrefaction, and imparting so grateful a quickness to the rest, as supplies the want of *Orange*, *Limon*, and other *Omphacia*, and therefore never to be excluded.

This salad green that ought "never to be excluded" from the salad bowl is rare in American salad bowls. There are still several *Rumex* cultivars grown on the Continent, but here we are fortunate to find any! Most common in our seed catalogs is *R. acetosa*, the broad-leaved perennial sorrel. Park Seed sells this as an herb, and both Le Jardin du Gourmet and Redwood City Seed offer the same cultivar, BELLEVILLE, much grown in France and Belgium. *R. patienta*, grown in some herb gardens as "patience," produces edible leaves several weeks before Belleville is potherb size and is available from Redwood City. *R. scutatus*, sometimes called garden sorrel, is smaller and more thrifty in habit than *R. acetosa*. *R. montanus*, or French sorrel is known in two forms—a smooth-leaved type and a crimp-leaved type, both excellent in salads and grown in France for use in omelets and as a bed puree for poached eggs. *R. crispus* is usually grown for its rust red decorative seed and much used in flower arrangements. Occasionally one of these sorrels can be found tucked away in an herb nursery's back gardens, and it is always worthwhile to ask after the less common small salad plants when browsing through a newly discovered herb nursery's beds.

The taste of cultivated sorrel is acid and tangy, but quite a bit milder than the wild sourgrass sorrel with its tiny spade-shaped leaves. Because sorrel leaves wilt very rapidly, it is almost never seen in produce markets and should not be picked until a few minutes before it is wanted in the salad. It is an outstanding source of vitamins A, B, and C, and iron.

Growing Sorrel

Sorrel is a perennial, and if set in the garden and allowed to go to seed, it can spread everywhere. Many salad gardeners give it its own bed away from the main garden, but I have never had any trouble keeping it in bounds, for I cut back the flower stalks that appear in midsummer. Sorrel has deep roots and appreciates a manure-rich, deeply worked, moist soil. The plants must be supplied with liberal amounts of water during dry spells or the leaves get tough.

The seed can be sown in autumn or very early spring. When the young plants are out of the seedling stage, they should be thinned to stand 12 to 14 inches apart. Each plant will form a many-leaved clump. Keeping the leaves harvested will keep the clumps producing. The outer leaves are the ones to pick while they are still young, leaving the new growth in the center to produce an ongoing supply. Sorrel tends to go to seed rapidly in hot dry weather, if allowed. Keep the flowering stalk cut back unless you want more young plants in the same bed next year. Every three or four years the clumps should be divided and set in another rich, sunny bed, or a new bed should be sown with seed. An old sorrel bed should be given over for several years to restorative cover crops, for *Rumex* is a heavy feeder and can exhaust the soil.

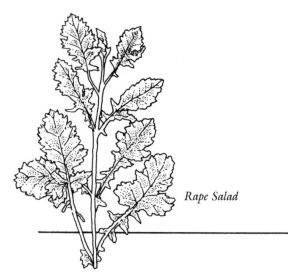

Rape Salad

Rape Salad *(Brassica napus)*

This is an ancient and modern fodder plant, best known for its oil, which is much used in cooking and salads. This plant is also a green manure crop used to renew exhausted soil. It is much planted in this country and Canada, but not many gardeners realize that its young green leaves are good both in salads or cooked like spinach.

Rape seed is available from Hastings, whose catalog describes it as the "cheapest and easiest of all greens to grow. Broadcast seed once a month and have fall, winter, and spring greens. . . ." Rape, which matures in 21 days, can also be grown in cold frames.

Roselle *(Hibiscus sabdariffa)*

Travelers to the Caribbean may enjoy delicious green salads made with roselle, or Jamaica sorrel. The plant is native to West Africa but became especially favored in Jamaica when it was introduced early in the eighteenth century. The tart, tender young leaves taste very much like sorrel and are used as a common ingredient in Caribbean salads. (The fleshy, juicy calyxes are also edible and are made into a refreshing drink, added to sauces, and used to flavor jellies.) I have not seen seed offered in any catalog, including those offering unusual tropical plants. Florida gardeners might be able to grow this tasty salad leaf.

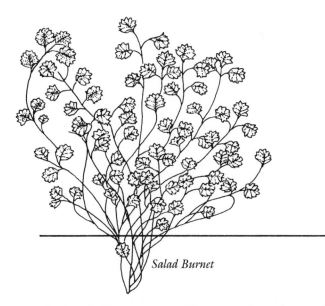

Salad Burnet

Salad Burnet *(Sanguisorba officinalis)*

This cucumber-flavored green of the Rose family, native to Europe and western Asia, has been cultivated since ancient times.

It grows in low clumps and looks a little like a robust maidenhair fern when glimpsed quickly out of the corner of one's eye. One of its common names is the pimpernel.

In ancient days, burnet had a medicinal use in salves and teas to help wounds heal faster, and it supposedly helped staunch bleeding. Traditionally a sprig of burnet was put in a glass of wine, not only to bolster the drinker's blood, but because it was "very delightful to the palate" as John Parkinson wrote in *Paradisi in Sole, Paradisus Terrestris*, in 1629. By Parkinson's time burnet had moved out of the medieval medicine chest and into the salad bowl where it was a favorite mixed with "other sallet herbes to give a finer relish thereunto." Thomas Jefferson planted burnet liberally in his gardens, and the beautiful plant was growing early on in the Colonies.

At the end of the nineteenth century, E. Lewis Sturtevant wrote in his *Notes*, "It is rarely cultivated in the garden but occurs in all our books on gardening." Even today burnet is listed in the herb sections of some seed catalogs, when it is found at all, and is grown in many flower gardens as an attractive, lacy-leaved edging, but it rarely makes it to the North American salad bowl. It should be better known for its delicate, fresh fragrance and cool cucumber taste, like very pure mountain spring water that seems to intensify the flavors of other salad ingredients. John Evelyn knew its virtues and quoted an Italian proverb celebrating the pimpernel in *Acetaria*, his treatise on salads:

L'Insalata non è buon, ne bella,
Ove non è la Pimpinella.

Loosely translated, this means "a salad is neither good nor beautiful unless it contains the pimpernel."

Growing Salad Burnet

Salad burnet is a deep-rooted perennial. It will stay green under the snow all winter and can be grown as an annual nearly everywhere. It likes best a dry, sandy, poor soil. Each spreading, rosette-shaped, rounded clump takes up to 12 to 14 inches of space in the garden. Two or three plants are enough for most salad lovers, but the attractiveness of the plant makes it a good one for edging.

In the early spring of its second year, salad burnet sends up wiry stems with fuzzy flower heads like pale pink caterpillars. Most gardeners cut these off in their eagerness to encourage thick foliage. Burnet, which will reseed itself, has also been planted as a forage crop for quail in the New Jersey Pine Barrens and in sections of California.

Burnet may be propagated by root division, but it is so easily grown from seed that division is something done only when a delighted dinner guest cries, "I must have some for my own salad garden." The seed may be directly sown in the garden in spring or late fall. Burnet dislikes rich, moist, acid soil, and finds a sandy soil with a nearly neutral pH ideal. Correct an acid soil before you grow burnet. The handsome seeds, with their diamond pattern, should be covered with a thin layer of sand, about ⅛ inch deep. The seed germinates in about ten days, and after the young plants are well developed, they can be thinned out to 10 to 12 inches apart unless you prefer a luxuriously thick border effect to hide the evidence of salad-leaf gathering.

Cold climate burnet lovers can mulch the plants in their first autumn for protection through the winter, then allow some plants to go to seed in the succeeding season so they will provide replacement stock for any that succumb to the cold.

To use burnet in salads, strip the leaves from a stem or two and blend them in with other salad greenery. The leaves can be used in sandwiches, in salad dressings (chopped fine), or in sour cream and yogurt dips. Fresh burnet is far superior to the dried or frozen article. A sprig of burnet is refreshing in summer drinks. (At one time burnet was an important ingredient in flavoring ale.) A handful of sprigs steeped in a good cider or pear vinegar makes a marvelous burnet vinegar. After the vinegar has steeped the leaves for several weeks to the desired strength, drain it off into a clean bottle and discard the soggy leaves.

Many seed houses offer *Sanguisorba minor* (listed in earlier books as *Poterium sanguisorba*) but J. L. Hudson offers *Sanguisorba officinalis*, or the great burnet, which grows as tall as 5 feet and has beautiful dark purple flowers. The young leaves are delicious in salads. Redwood City Seed has BURNET SAXIFRAGE (*Pimpinella saxifraga*) whose young leaves have a similar cucumber taste and are good in salads.

John Evelyn added an interesting note on *Sanguisorba minor* used as one would use the spice pepper, in his *Acetaria*. "And here let me mention the *Root* of the *Minor Pimpinella*, or small *Burnet saxifrage*, which being dried, is by some extoll'd beyond all other *Peppers*, and more wholsom."

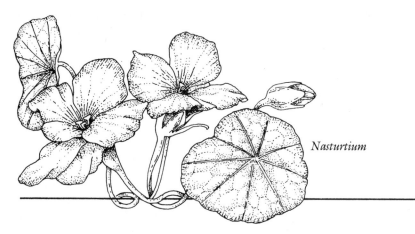

Nasturtium

Nasturtium *(Tropaeolum majus* and *T. minus)*

John Parkinson called the nasturtium by its liveliest name, YELLOW LARK'S HEELS. Other cultivars are known by the less poetic names of CREEPING CANARY, INDIAN CRESS, and SCOTCH FLAME-FLOWER. It is a native of the cool, high mountains from Mexico to Chile and was one of the most exciting plant discoveries of the sixteenth century, arriving in Europe, as so many tropical beauties did, by way of Spain. Wrote John Gerard in his *Herbal*:

The seeds of this rare and faire plant came first from the Indies into Spaine and those hot regions, and from thence into France and Flanders, from whence I have received seeds that hath borne with me both flowers and seeds.

The nasturtium Gerard knew was *Tropaeolum minus*, similar to our familiar *T. majus* (introduced into England in 1684) writes plant historian Alice M. Coats in her *Flowers and Their Histories* (1968, 1971), but "whose yellow flowers are characterized by a small but distinct point to each petal and a purplish splash on the three lower ones. This species was afterwards lost, and though reintroduced late in the eighteenth century and popularized for a time, has again more or less disappeared."

The earliest description of a nasturtium was written by the Spanish physician Monardes, who referred to it as "Floures of Blood," and wrote, "I sowed a seede which thei brought me from the Peru, more to see his fairnesse, than for any medicinall vertues that it hath. It is a flour very beautiful, which doth adornate the gardens."

Nasturtium was one of the first flowers planted in the garden of the Governor's Palace in Williamsburg in 1698 as a rare and beautiful plant. By 1806 Bernard M'Mahon listed nasturtium in his seed catalog. As the pioneers moved west, the nasturtium went with them, for its adaptability, easy culture, and bright jewellike flowers. Discoveries of new nasturtiums in Chile and Patagonia in the nineteenth century led to many experiments in hybridization, one of which was the TOM THUMB dwarf variety that enjoyed immediate success. The original scented, semi-double GOLDEN GLEAM nasturtium was discovered by California nurseryman J. C. Bolgier in 1928, and it took an international prize at the Chelsea Garden Show in 1931. Gleam is still listed in our catalogs along with many hybrids stressing double flowers and an abundance of regular-shaped lark's heels. (The older varieties had more leaves and fewer, irregularly shaped flowers.)

Nasturtium leaves and flowers and seed pods have been used in salads almost as soon as the plant arrived in salad-loving Europe. William Cobbett, of course, made his usual nasty dig when he described nasturtiums as "an annual plant, with a half-red half-yellow flower, which has an offensive smell . . . the better the ground the fewer of them are necessary." John Evelyn puts nasturtiums in his salads, but lumped them along with the garden cresses and watercress as "moderately hot, and aromatick, quicken the torpent Spirits, and purge the Brain, and are of singular effect against the *Scorbute*. Both the tender Leaves, *Calices*, *Cappuchin Capers*, and *Flowers*, are laudably mixed with the colder Plants.

The *Buds* being Candy'd, are likewise us'd in Strewings all Winter."

There are something like fifty species in the solitary *Tropaeolum* genus. The family classification is Tropaeolaceae, from the Greek word for "trophy" because the round leaves look like tiny shields. *Nasturtium* is a marvelous Latin word meaning "the nose-twisting thing." Most of these species are vigorous climbers. English gardens, with their cool summers and mild winters often feature perennial climbing nasturtiums, the *majus*. A nineteenth-century American garden writer described the climbers as "excellent . . . for quickly covering up and concealing any unsightly place." The plants are not suited to hot climates despite their blazing flowers. *Minus* is a sprawling, semihardy annual, and the flowers of both *majus* and *minus* are used in salads in conjunction with other greens for their peppery taste and handsome appearance.

Growing Nasturtium

Nasturtium flowers are brilliantly attractive in the salad garden, and the plant is a rapid grower. It does best in a light, sandy soil low in nitrogen, as does salad burnet. In the North, nasturtium is grown in full sun, but in the South it must have a cooler, shaded environment.

The plants grow well from either seeds or cuttings. Sow the seed where the plants are wanted in the garden when the soil temperature reaches 65°F. Cover the seeds with half an inch of fine, sifted soil. They will germinate in a week to ten days, and will bloom about six weeks later. Nasturtiums will go to much leaf and little flower if grown in rich, well-manured soil, but that doesn't bother the salad maker who wants as many of the little shield-shaped leaves as possible. The plants may also be started indoors in a cool place and transplanted outside or grown in pots.

Autumn cuttings, about 4 inches long, inserted in sand or perlite will root and may be potted and brought into a sunny window for winter salads. Cut the young growing tips of a plant for salads.

Aphids are sometimes pastured on nasturtiums by ants. Cedo-Flora poured into the ants' tunnels may persuade them to take their aphids somewhere else. Controlling the ants is the secret of controlling the aphids.

Midsummer Nasturtium Salad

4 cups or so mixed lettuces, corn salad, young chicory, or endive
1 cup nasturtium leaves
2 hard-cooked eggs, peeled and quartered
   oil and vinegar dressing
½ cup nasturtium flowers

Wash and spin-dry the leaves. Chill in the refrigerator until crisp and cold. Add the eggs and dressing and mix gently in a bowl. Garnish with the nasturtium flowers and serve.

4 servings

Nasturtium leaves and flowers are delicious in salads and both are also good in thin tea sandwiches. The smaller, more tender leaves are best. The largest leaves can be stuffed like vine leaves with any suitable filling, and then cooked, after they are tied up with twine. Nasturtium vinegar is made by steeping the new flowers not yet fully opened in a good-quality salad vinegar for several weeks, either alone or in company with garlic and herbs. The vinegar is drained into a fresh bottle when the flavor is right.

Almost everything written on the nasturtium for the last three centuries extols the pickled seed pods as an excellent substitute for the expensive imported capers, the pickled buds of *Capparis spinosa*. Indeed, I have pickled them myself, and they were very good. But recently, herbalist Gertrude B. Foster and Rosemary F. Louden in their book, *Park's Success with Herbs*, warn us against the pickled nasturtium pod:

A modern doctor told us that the seeds contain oxalic acid in sufficient quantity, considering their volume, to make it inadvisable to pickle them for a caper substitute or eat them raw. However, the flowers and leaves do not have even a microscopic quantity of it.

And, although I have never grown it myself, I understand that the real caper bush, *C. spinosa*, is a tender perennial native to the more arid Mediterranean region and can be grown here as an annual. It has showy, beautiful, big flowers whose buds are pickled to make capers. Finding the seed is the puzzler.

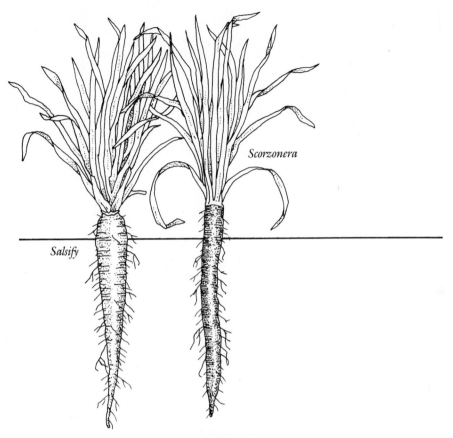

Salsify *(Tragopogan porrifolius)*

Quite a few gardeners grow the oyster plant, as salsify is known, for the delicious, mild roots, but how many realize that the young, tender, grasslike leaves are good in salads, and have a sweet, agreeable taste? If you already grow salsify, try adding a few leaves to your early salads.

Scorzonera *(Scorzonera hispanica)*

Scorzonera is very much underrated here as a vegetable, but the black-skinned cylindrical roots are delicious when cooked, and one of the scorzoneras, French scorzonera, or *picridie* as it's called in France, is grown in France and Belgium as a wonderful cut-and-come-again salad green with a unique flavor. The Urban

Farmer offers these root scorzoneras whose young leaves may be added to the salad dish—two cultivars from Holland where the plant is esteemed—one, an improved type called PONORA VER-BETERDE REUZEN NIETSCHIETERS, and the other, resistant to bolting, EENJARIGE NIETSCHIETERS TRIPLEX. A third type is a French strain of the old GIANT BLACK RUSSIAN. All three come in a sampler packet, though separately packed so the seed won't be mixed, a common offering of The Urban Farmer, which realizes gardeners like to compare cultivars of the same vegetable.

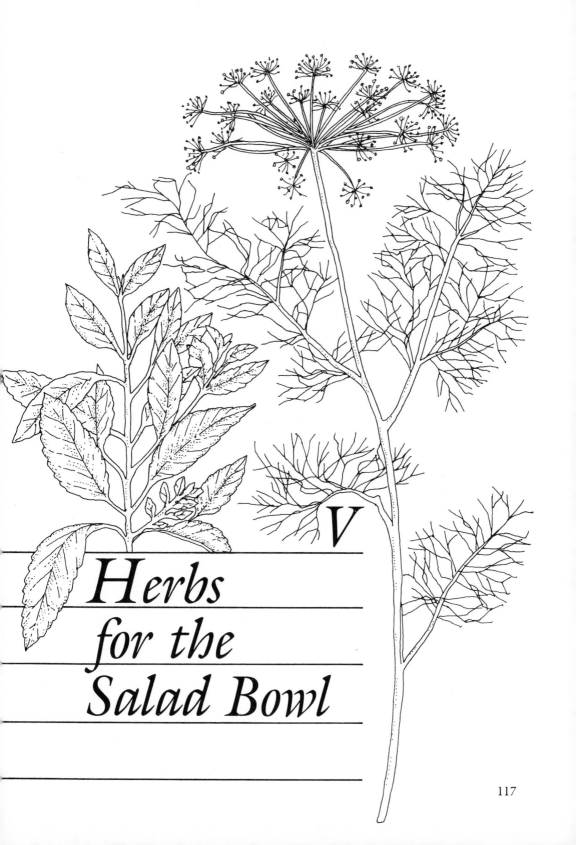

V

Herbs for the Salad Bowl

*T*here are times when even the most assiduously cultivated gardens offer a scanty variety for the salad bowl—two or three types of lettuce, perhaps an escarole or chicory head. At such desperate moments the lackluster personality of the salad can be greatly enlivened with a few well-chosen herbs, either added in leaf form to the body of the salad, or chopped fine and beaten into the dressing for a more subtle distribution of flavors. The strong aromatic oils in most herbs make it prudent to use them in salads with careful discrimination. Nothing is more daunting than to bite a powerfully flavored herb leaf in what seemed to be a pleasant mouthful of salad, so always mince herbs very finely or simply rub them into the bowl for a less brash effect. There are a few herbs that are so excellent in salads that a handful can be used—the tender tips of the milder mints are wonderfully refreshing in hot weather, and parsley can be used quite liberally if it is tender and not too curly in texture. Beware the tight-curled parsleys, which give the disagreeable sensation of vegetable wool in the mouth! The Italian flat-leaved parsley finds more favor in salads.

An herb garden near the kitchen door (or on the windowsill) where the cook can nip outside and gather the necessaries in a few seconds is ideal, for correction of the balance of flavors in the salad can be made on the spot. The salad herbs listed below are used as leaves or flowers in the salad bowl, as flavorings for vinegar, and as major ingredients in salad dressings. Dressings, whether creamy or oil-and-vinegar types, tend to mollify and soften the more violent flavors of herbs, so reserve strong-tasting leaves for the dressing bottle.

Sweet Basil *(Ocimum basilicum)*

A fragrant, aromatic plant, with about 150 subspecies, and from the warmer sections of the temperate or tropical zones, sweet basil has been used in kitchens since the most ancient times. Some curious practices were once linked with the growing of sweet basil—Romans cursed and swore when they planted the seed under the impression that the more richly basil was reviled the better it grew. When a good crop was wanted, as soon as the seeds were sown the gardener would grind it underfoot and pray earnestly to the gods that the thing would not vegetate; but basil, being contrary in nature, responded with abundant growth.

Basil was thought to destroy the sight if one ate greatly of it, and medieval authorities thought it good against scorpion stings. Over the centuries a grand list of virtues and cautions associated with basil grew up, but the one of greatest interest here is John Evelyn's gentle advice in *Acetaria*: "Basil, *Ocimum* (as Basil), imparts a grateful flavour, if not too strong, somewhat offensive to the Eyes, and therefore the tender Tops to be sparingly used in our Sallet."

This tender annual is at home in the salad garden or in a windowsill pot, and it makes a handsome bed edging. There are scores of sweet basil cultivars listed in herb garden literature, but it's rare to find more than a handful in our seed catalogs. Some gardeners have found it an absorbing hobby to seek out and collect the basils by studying special catalogs, joining herb societies, visiting new nurseries at vacation time or on trips, and following the basil news in the several herb growers' magazines.

Some of the basils are grown for medicinal teas, some for use as insect repellents, others for potpourris and scented herbal wreaths, for decorative borders, and for culinary uses, including the steeped leaves to flavor vinegar and the fresh young leaves in salads.

Sweet basil needs a long season to mature, and it is grown commercially in California where it is sown directly in the field. Gardeners in colder climates should start their basil seeds inside at least six weeks before the last killing frosts, or plan to grow the aromatic herb in pots under lights, where it will do very well.

Basil germinates at about 70°F and does not tolerate temperature fluctuations in its shift from flat to cold frame to garden, so care must be taken to keep the progress from seed packet to herb bed as smooth and even in temperature as possible.

Plants in the garden should be set out or thinned to 12 inches apart and placed where they will be in the full sun, yet sheltered from chilling winds. Each plant can burgeon to a height of 24 inches with profuse branching, so leave room. The rich, somewhat bitter odor of basil in full sunlight and the somnolent humming of bees are two of the characteristics of the late summer garden.

You may use the leaves of basil for salads at any time in the plant's growth after the seedling stage, but remember that the small, young leaves are the tenderest.

At the end of the summer, it is possible to pot up a few basil plants and bring them inside for continued use and enjoyment, but take care to choose a good large pot and to transplant in the evening after a thorough watering when the shock will be less. Transplanted basils faint and wilt when handled roughly, despite the old Roman adjuration to trample them for their own good.

Other interesting basils for the salad gardener are lettuce leaf basil and lemon basil.

Sweet Basil

Lemon Basil

Lettuce Leaf Basil

Lettuce Leaf Basil *(Ocimum basilicum* var. *crispum)*

This handsome basil produces large leaves—3 to 4 inches long—and it is the one most often used in making pesto. If you enjoy the inimitable pungency of basil in salads *(lente, lente!)* perhaps to accompany an Italian menu, try this big-leaved type cut or torn into snippets and mixed with a blander gathering of lettuces.

Lettuce leaf basil needs a lot of space, as much as 18 inches between plants. The leaves of one plant should not touch those of a neighbor lest the plant's special drainage system for shedding rain and morning dew be thwarted. Cold water on the leaves can cause black spots, so take care when giving thirsty basil plants a drink. Drip irrigation or a half-buried coffee can with holes punched in the bottom are better ways to water than sprinklers, whether automatic or hand held.

Lettuce leaf basil does not take to potting up at the end of the season very well, and it is better to start a plant or two in pots and keep them there rather than try to shift a big plant out of its garden home and into the confines of a house pot.

Lemon Basil *(Ocimum basilicum* var. *citriodorum)*

This basil, according to herb authority Gertrude B. Foster, was introduced to the United States in 1940 from Thailand by the United States Department of Agriculture (USDA), but it seems to have been known and grown in England in the sixteenth century and is mentioned by the classic garden writers.

Lemon basil has the reputation of being harder to grow than the other basils, and it does not transplant well, for it has a tendency to bolt to seed right after it is set out, presumably from transplant shock. One remedy is to sow the seed in a shallow furrow in the permanent place you intend for the plants after the soil is thoroughly warm. Cover the seed with very fine sifted soil half an inch deep and press the soil down firmly with a short length of board. When the seedlings are well up, thin them out to leave 8 to 10 inches between plants.

The leaves of lemon basil are fewer and sparser than other basils. To use them in salads, cut a few stems and strip off the leaves; chop them fine before adding to the salad.

Redwood City Seed has a very nice collection of sweet basils— the ITALIAN LARGE-LEAVED; the SMALL BUSH; DARK OPAL *(purpurascens)*, with purple leaves much used in vinegar; LETTUCE LEAF; NAPOLETANO; and PICOLLO. Both Napoletano and Picollo are Italian basils, obviously, and the herb is closely linked with the finest Italian cuisines. It is also an essential ingredient in *pistou*, a popular garlicky-tasting soup of Provence. Redwood City also lists the SMALL-LEAVED GREEN basil, a type highly suited to pot culture. A search through the specialty catalogs will reward the basil lover with many others.

Bergamot

Bergamot (*Monarda* spp.)

This group of plants—known also as bee balm, horsemint, and Oswego tea—are large, coarse annuals and perennials native to North America. They seem to have been designed especially for hummingbirds, having long red tube-shaped florets arranged in a ragged twist around the center. Some varieties have pink or white, lavender or maroon flowers. Both the leaves and the florets can be used in salads. The leaves, when steeped, make an exquisitely fragrant tea, and it is the bergamot in Earl Grey tea that gives it such a fine bouquet.

Bergamot makes a large, handsome background for a border, for it grows up to 3 feet tall with its striking cluster of flowers that endure for a long time and attract hummingbirds and bees. It is a good idea to grow enough to satisfy your eyes, the salad bowl, the birds, and the bees.

Monarda didyma likes a moist, loamy, acid soil. It can be started by seed inside and set out after the last frosts about 12 inches between plants in the permanent bed. Bergamot seems to like full sun, but can stand some shade. After the plants flower, they send out runners from the mother clump and expand their territory. A good layer of compost should be added to bergamot beds in the late autumn; it serves as a winter mulch and a spring tonic.

There are a number of *Monarda* species growing wild in North America, and the leaves and flowers of all are good in salads, though their principal use is in teas. *M. didyma*, from which the cultivated types came, is found wild in moist woods, along streambanks and in thickets from Michigan to New York and southward to Tennessee and Georgia where its habitat tends to be in the higher elevations. Other bergamots are *M. fistulosa* var. *menthifolia*, which is sold in open-air markets in New Mexico and Arizona as oregano, which it very closely resembles!

A mixture of many shades of red, crimson, pink, and scarlet is available from Nichols Garden Nursery and J. L. Hudson as well as others.

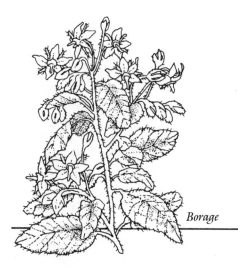

Borage

Borage *(Borago officinalis)*

A large, lusty annual plant, borage has hairy leaves and stems and fine, bright blue flowers that make a good show. The plant is happy to reseed itself, and gardeners are happy to have it do so.

Borage is of Mediterranean origin and grows now all over the world. Its common names are cool-tankard and talewort. The ancient Greeks and Romans used borage in their drinks to make a cooling beverage. Says E. Lewis Sturtevant about borage:

The Greeks called it *euphrosynon*, for, when put in a cup of wine, it made those who drank it merry. It has been used in England since the days of Parkinson. In Queen Elizabeth's time, both the leaves and flowers were eaten in salads. It is at present cultivated for use in cooling drinks and is used by some as a substitute for spinach. The leaves contain so much nitre that when dry they burn like match paper. The leaves also serve as a garnish and are likewise pickled. . . . Borage is enumerated by Peter Martyr as among the plants cultivated at Isabela Island by the companions of Columbus. It appears in the catalogs of our American seedsmen and is mentioned by almost all of the earlier writers of gardening. The flowering parts of borage are noted or figured by nearly all of the ancient herbalists.

Herbalists and old medicinal plant manuals claim many virtues for borage, and the plant seems to have been universally esteemed. John Gerard says in his *Herbal*, "Those of our time do use the floures in sallads, to exhilerate and make the mind glad. There be also many things made of them, used everywhere for the comfort of the heart, for the driving away of sorrow, and encreasing the joy of the minde." Our friend, John Evelyn, the salad champion, remarks, "The tender Leaves and Flowers especially, may be eaten in Composition; but above all, the Sprigs in Wine, like those of Baum, are of known Vertue to revive the Hypochondriac, and chear the hard Student."

Modern gardeners find that the thought of those hairy leaves in a salad make them balk, but the flowers and scraped stems are excellent in the salad dish. They have a cooling, cucumbery taste. Borage sprigs are still very much used in refreshing midsummer drinks—Pimm's Cup, for one. Experimenters will find that the very young leaves of borage, not yet cushioned in down, are a pleasant addition to salads. Borage is supposed to give one who eats it courage, and an ancient rhyme goes "I, Borage, always bring Courage."

Add the blue flowers to salads for a charming effect and pleasant taste. Cut a few stems for salad use, also, but scrape off the shining hairs, rinse and pat dry before slicing them into the salad.

Plant the large seeds directly in the garden early in the year. Borage seedlings can take some light frost. Thin the plants out to 15 inches apart. The plant grows up to 3 feet tall and should be set in a sheltered, sunny location. If they are exposed to heavy winds and rain, they may have to be staked. I had a large clump of borage laid flat by a midsummer thunderstorm, and they stayed recumbent for the rest of the growing season.

Flowers in Your Salads

The flowers of many plants are edible and can make the simplest green salad an exquisite gustatory bouquet. But salad fanciers should not blindly strew their salads with any flower that looks good—many plants are poisonous; choose flowers only of edible plants or those listed in a competent source.

One of the best guides for using flowers in the salad bowl is the section on wild and domestic flowers in English garden writer Joy Larkcom's very fine book, *The Salad Garden* (1984). Larkcom suggests using the leaves and flowers of geraniums, pelargoniums, and lavender; the petals of roses, marigolds, and borage; and the flowers and buds of hollyhocks and nasturtiums—and more.

Chive blossoms are a dramatic addition to a salad, and calendula petals scattered through a tossed salad give it a vivacity and brilliance that is quite unusual. Apple blossoms are very beautiful, and one of the few flowers with a distinctive and excellent taste is the flower of the blueberry. Wild huckleberry or blueberry bushes can yield a handful or so of these good, slightly acid little blossoms. Dandelion petals pulled loose from the head give a salad a touch of shining gold, as do the blossoms of the wild mustards. If you use flowers with a lumpy central knot, such as daisies or hollyhocks, be sure to separate the soft petal from the harder section—eating flowers should be an evanescent experience unmarred by the crunch of solid parts.

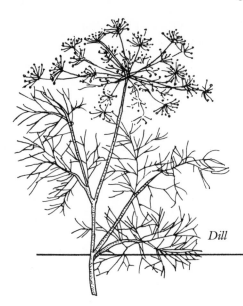

Dill

Dill *(Anethum graveolens)*

Dill is an annual or biennial member of the *Umbelliferae*, native to the old world. The fine, thready leaves and distinctive flavor are familiar to most people. The flowers and seeds as well as the leaves are used in salads and to flavor sauces and pickles. In the northern central and eastern European countries—Russia, Hungary, Poland, Scandinavia—dill is used extensively, while in France it is ignored and hardly known. The Italians, for whom everything has salad possibilities, use it in a *saladini* mixture, and it is very good, cut fine and sprinkled through a green salad. The leaves, flowers or seeds may be used to make a steeped dill vinegar.

The seeds of dill used to be given to restless children to quiet them down in the long hours of church in early days and were called "meeting house seeds." Dill was also thought to control witches' activities, and an old rhyme went:

> Vervain and dill
> Hinder witches of their will.

It was considered a good hiccup cure, and Ann Leighton in *Early American Gardens* quotes an old translation of Dioscorides advising that a decoction of dill "stayeth the yeox, hicet, or hisquet."

The plant matures in about 70 days, but the salad gardener can clip it any time after it has reached some size. It is a fast-growing, fairly hardy plant that should be sown in early spring in well-prepared fine soil. When the plants are 4 to 5 inches high, thin them to stand a foot apart. They will grow 3 feet tall and more.

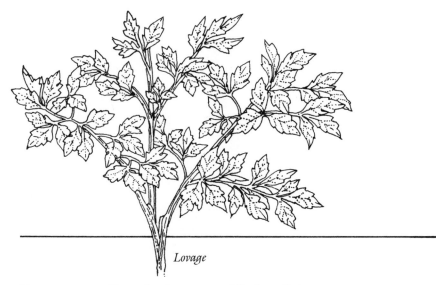

Lovage

Lovage *(Levisticum officinale)*

Lovage inclines toward being a kind of sweet, aromatic celery with oriental overtones and a warming, pungent taste in the mouth. Its rich green, toothed leaves make it a handsome plant in the salad garden and a striking ornamental in the border.

The leaves and tenderest stems are good in all salads, as well as soups and sauces. The Romans of the present day still use lovage a good deal in their cookery. Salads with lovage are superb accompaniments to fresh salmon or bluefish.

The plant is a long-lived perennial (though it needs autumn mulching in the North), and the flower stems with their "spoky tufts" as John Gerard wrote, can grow up to 6 feet tall given the rich, moist soil they like. The flower stalks may be cut back to prevent seeding.

Lovage can be started indoors in flats six to eight weeks before the frosts end. Two or three plants are plenty for the average salad maker's summer needs, and the hardy plants will endure in their bed for many years. Gerard recommended all the parts of the lovage plant. The roots, he said, "are good for all inward diseases." The seed aided digestion and spiced up meats, and water distilled with lovage "cleareth the sight, and putteth away all spots, . . . freckles . . . and redness of the face, if they be often washed therewith."

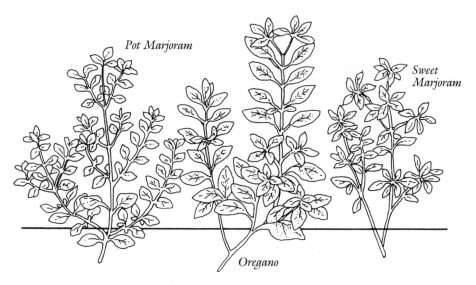

Pot Marjoram

Sweet Marjoram

Oregano

Sweet Marjoram *(Origanum majorana)*
Pot Marjoram *(O. onites)*
Oregano *(O. vulgare)*

There are fifteen to twenty species of *Origanum*, and half a dozen are familiars in the herb garden, usually grown as tender annuals. Sweet marjoram, oregano, and pot marjoram are the most common. They are all too highly flavored to be used as fresh leaves in salads, though rubbing a wooden salad bowl with sprigs of the leaves or chopping a few leaves very finely into the dressing adds ineffable bouquet to a salad. All can be grown in pots on the windowsill.

In early days the marjorams had an honored place in the pharmacopoeia. Decoctions, powders, and potions made with the various marjorams were good against "the bitings and stingings of venomous beasts," according to Gerard. They also mitigated the effects of opium or poison hemlock, worked against lung congestion and coughs, healed wounds over, calmed seasickness, and, in the bargain, drove away serpents. The extracted oil was believed to make joints supple when rubbed into the skin.

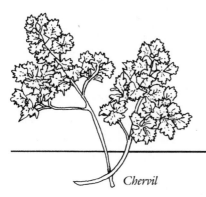

Chervil

Chervil *(Anthriscus cerefolium)*
Sweet Cicely *(Myrrhis odorata)*

The Greek name for chervil, *chairephyllon*, means "herb of joy," and the fragrant annual or biennial from the Caucasus and northern Europe is an ancient plant that has gone into salads for centuries. It was known to the Greeks and other Mediterranean peoples far back in the mists of time. It is a spring or autumn crop that does best in cool weather and can be snipped into salads six weeks or so after the seeds are sown.

Its mild, aromatic flavor made John Evelyn write that chervil should be in every salad, that it was good for one, especially for "chearing the spirits." John Gerard liked the aromatic seeds in his salads "dressed as the cunning Cooke knoweth how. . . ." and wrote in the *Herbal* that "eaten in sallads when they are green, with oil and vinegar, by the agreeableness of their taste, are better than other sallads through the sweetness of their aroma, and nothing is healthier for weak stomachs." As for the leaves, they are "exceeding good, wholesome and pleasant among other sallad herbs, giving the taste of Annise-seed unto the rest."

There is some confusion as to whether these old writers were referring to *Anthriscus cerefolium* or sweet cicely *(Myrrhis odorata)*. Both are good in salads.

Anthriscus cerefolium is a hardy annual with delicate, lacy leaves that add much to a salad. The French use this extensively in *bouquets garni*, to season omelets and to add piquancy to salads. It is somewhat more bitter than *Myrrhis odorata*. This cultivar prefers a cool, shady section of the garden and will rapidly bolt to seed if grown in a dry, sunny location. The flower is similar to that of parsley and sweet fennel.

Sow seed in the bed in early spring for a summer crop, or in late summer for a mulched, overwintered crop that will produce delicious leaves early in the spring. It also makes a good windowsill potherb.

Myrrhis odorata is a hardy perennial even more fernlike in appearance than *Anthriscus cerefolium*, and it has fuzzier leaves. In some regions it is called giant chervil, for the flower stalks, bearing large, lacy white umbels, tower 4 to 6 feet high. It makes a handsome background border or foundation planting as long as the location is cool and shady, and the soil has a rich composition similar to that enjoyed by woodland plants.

The seed of *Myrrhis odorata* needs cold treatment or it must be allowed to lie in place in its bed over winter before it will germinate. Established plants have deep taproots and are hard to transplant. Seed may be ordered from J. L. Hudson.

Chervil

Batty Langley in *New Principles of Gardening*, written in 1728, offers some advice on growing chervil.

Chervil being an excellent Sallet Herb, is still to be cultivated, but need not be sown upon old decayed hot Beds under Glasses, &c. as before. The Season being now warm enough for its Growth in the natural Borders, as the heat of the Spring advances, make choice of such Borders to sow your Seed in, as are not so fully exposed to the heat, as a *South* Border.

When you find your young Salleting begins to start, or run away as soon as out of Ground, then remove your place of raising to some *East* border, which the Sun will depart from about eleven in the Morning, and your Salleting will be much finer; and whenever you find that in very hot weather your Salleting begins to run, as before in the *South* Border, then remove to a *North* border, wherein you may raise it with Pleasure.

Ann Leighton remarks in *Early American Gardens* on a wild sweet cicely *(Osmorhiza longistylis)* that grows in New England where it is known as sweet jarvil, though few other writers take notice of the plant. *Hortus Third* notes that it grows from Quebec to Georgia and Texas.

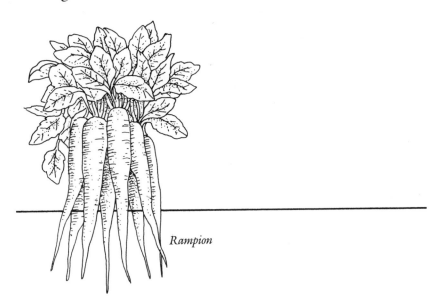

Rampion

Rampion *(Campanula rapunculus)*

Rampion leaves, smooth and shining, were once much used in salads, but few American gardeners today know the plant, and the seed is quite difficult to find here. It is something of an event when it does show up in a catalog every once in a while. Redwood City Seed offers it at a dollar a packet.

The plant is a biennial, with handsome blue bell-shaped flowers like its relatives, the flower garden campanulas, but the *Campanula rapunculus* leaves are smoother and more palatable. Both leaves and the roots are good in salads. The root has a walnutlike flavor and can be used raw or cooked and chilled. Rampion is still grown in many German, French, and Italian gardens and is most familiar to us, not in the salad bowl, but through the Grimm Brothers story of Rapunzel ("Rampion"), where a wife looked longingly over the wall into a witch's garden where a bed of fine rampion grew. In response to her pleading, at last the husband climbed over the wall and gathered a handful for her, "cost what it may." The following describes what happened:

She . . . ate it very eagerly. It was so very, very nice that the next day her longing for it increased threefold. She could have no peace unless her husband fetched her some more. So in the twilight he set out again, but when he got over the wall he was terrified to see the witch before him.

The witch, of course, demands their firstborn child, who turns out to be Rapunzel of the golden hair.

Herb authorities Gertrude B. Foster and Rosemary F. Louden in *Park's Success with Herbs* consider rampion to be "a collector's item among herb growers. . . . We cherish every self-sown specimen lest it be the last one grown in our garden." They recommend sowing the fresh-gathered, extremely fine seed in late summer in a flat at soil temperatures of 65 to 72°F and warns that germination is slow. The seed should not be covered over. Plants are thinned to about 8 inches apart in the sandy but well-watered rampion bed. The following spring the fresh leaves can be gathered for salads, but the gardener pays a price for this rare treat—no flowers.

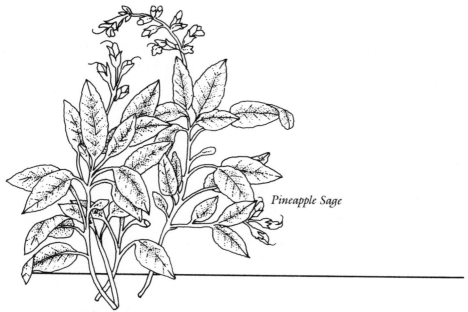

Pineapple Sage

Pineapple Sage *(Salvia elegans)*

There are hundreds of salvias, distributed all over the world, and the gardener who sets out to collect this group has a formidable task if he or she wishes to complete the set! Pineapple sage, a native of Mexico, is grown here as an annual and has a delightful fragrance of spice and pineapple. In Mexico it is a perennial, but in other locations it is treated as an annual. In northern gardens the season is not long enough to permit the plant to put out its crimson flowers.

The flavor of a delicious, fruity "pineapple" mixed with a mild sage taste makes it very pleasant in salads. Both the leaves and flowers can be used. If you live far enough south for the plants to flower you will find they attract both honeybees and hummingbirds.

Pineapple sage is easy to grow and produces an abundance of aromatic leaves. Plants are available from many herb growers around the country. Windowsill gardeners will be pleased to find that their sage plants will bloom indoors. Cuttings root quite easily in sand or growing medium.

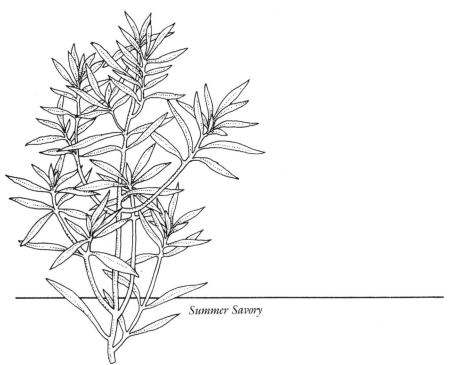

Summer Savory

Summer Savory *(Satureja hortensis)*

Summer savory is a hardy annual, while winter savory *(Satureja montana)* is a perennial (I have had a winter savory clump growing in central Vermont for five years). Summer savory is the better of the two for salads, since the leaf is more tender and a little milder, but it should be used in very small quantities— perhaps no more than a half teaspoon of leaves chopped very fine and mixed well with other greens. It is particularly good in three-bean salads and potato salads, and complements thyme in salad dressing mixtures.

The ancients set store by summer savory as a medicine to control flatulence, and, remarked John Gerard, was "with good successe boiled and eaten with beans, peason, and other windie pulses." Half an ounce of summer savory is included in John Winthrop, Jr.'s seed list.

Summer savory will self-sow, or may be started indoors six weeks before the frosts end. It is set outside in the garden after frost danger is past, with 12 inches or so between plants.

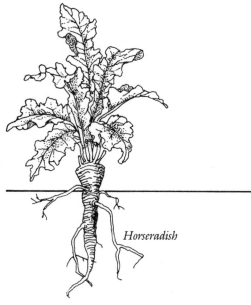

Horseradish

Horseradish *(Armoracia rusticana)*

Horseradish, a native of southeastern Europe, has been enjoyed since prehistoric times. Today the French eat the root raw in thin slices as an appetizer, and the grated root is sold in every supermarket in the United States to accompany roast beef and other bland meats. Most gardeners plant a rich bed with a few

roots for home-grated, fiery horseradish, which is put up with
vinegar and used in fish and meat sauces. Horseradish is consumed in enormous amounts in Germany. Yet how many gardeners know that the young leaves of horseradish plants, picked
early in the season, are a delicious addition to the salad bowl?
The young leaves are neither as hot nor as pungent as the root,
nor unpleasantly strong, but give a green salad a delicate snap
and verve unequaled by any other leaf. Only the young, pale
green leaves should be used, for as the leaves mature they get
too tough and leathery to be enjoyed. If you grow fond of horse-
radish-leaf salad, try blanching a few plants under an overturned
clay pot in early spring. Serve the resulting pale, tender leaf hearts
dressed with fine oil and vinegar enlivened only by a few snippets
of chives.

Horseradish does not mature viable seed. The plant is propagated by root cuttings, which are best planted in the early spring
and harvested in the fall. The plant is a heavy feeder, and it is
good gardening to rotate a soil builder into the horseradish bed
after a crop has been taken. Do not allow horseradish to go over
a second year.

Mace *(Achillea decolorans)*

This member of the yarrows is also known as smooth yarrow.
It is mentioned by Gertrude B. Foster and Rosemary F. Louden
in their *Park's Success with Herbs* as a recent import to this country
but grown in England for salad use under the name mace. The
plant, which is hardy in New England, must be grown from
divisions. It is a handsome, tooth-leaved clump like a handful
of flexible green saw blades. Assiduous searching through nursery
stock is necessary to find this unusual plant.

The yarrows are hardy perennials that grow easily in almost
any sunny garden soils. The plants have an ancient history of
staunching blood, easing migraine headaches, healing wounds,
halting hair loss, and mitigating the pain of toothache. The many
other yarrows that we grow in our garden borders or find escaped
to the wild are both too rough in texture and too strong in flavor
to use in salads, despite their fascinating history in home medicine
and their extraordinary hardiness. Perhaps the most charming

custom associated with the yarrows is the practice in late medieval times of eating yarrow at weddings to ensure the couple would love each other at least seven years.

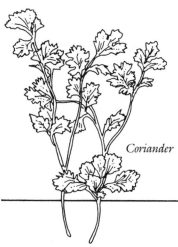

Coriander

Coriander *(Coriandrum sativum)*

This easily grown, airy plant is also called cilantro or Chinese parsley, even though it originated in the Mediterranean salad bowl in far distant times. It is a hardy annual that self-sows even in the North. It is an important plant in the cuisines of India, the oriental countries, Mexico, and South American countries and has become a chic fresh green plant in the produce sections of specialty food stores. It is a most useful plant in the garden, for insects dislike its scent, and it extends some measure of protection to nearby plants the pests find more alluring.

The spicy, strongly scented leaves have been used in salads in China, the Middle East, North Africa, Spain, Madagascar, Portugal, Cyprus, and several Latin American countries, but North American salad makers might take caution to add the leaves to their salads most sparingly unless they are habituated to the strong scent and pungency of coriander.

Grow coriander by seeding directly in the garden where the plants will grow in the spring. Plant them in a shallow furrow and cover lightly with fine soil or sand. Thin them to 4 to 6 inches apart. Make several sowings for a longer supply, for the plant goes to seed rather quickly. It is a good windowsill herb for winter salads.

Hops

Hops *(Humulus lupulus)*

The Latin name translates as "wolf hops" because, according to Waverly Root in *Food*, wild hops among other plants were as wolves in a sheepfold, rampant, rabid growers. The more ornamental cultivars are a fast way to shade an exposed porch. The good old common hop, a climbing vine that shoots up to 18 feet, was introduced here from Europe very early and soon escaped into the byways and hedges. It has been used to raise bread, flavor beer (its best-known use), and to make a medicinal tea believed to cleanse the blood of ill humours.

Some writers have described the hop sprouts as good and cheap, and very pleasant in salads. John Gerard wrote, "The buds or first sprouts which come forth in the spring are used to be eaten in sallads; yet are they, as Pliny saith, more toothsome than nourishing." In 1574, Reynolde Scot, writing the first book on hops, declared:

> There will some smell out the profitable savour of this herb, some wyll gather the fruit thereof, and will make a sallet therewith (which is good in one respect for the bellye, and in another for the Purse), and when the grace and sweetnesse

thereof conceived, some will dippe their fingers therein up to the knuckles, and some will be glad to licke the Dish, and they that disdayne to be partaken hereof, commonly prove to be such as have montaynes in fantasie, and beggary in possession.

But John Evelyn, that champion and connoisseur of salads, thought hops "hot and moist, rather Medicinal than fit for a Sallet, the Buds and young Tendrels excepted." In some parts of the world today, the young shoots and tendrils are still thought to be a delicacy and a rare salad, especially in Belgium and parts of Germany where the hop season brings these special salads to the table as well as side dishes of creamed hop shoots, much as Vermonters and Maine down-easters enjoy fiddlehead fern shoots for a brief week or two each spring.

The seeds of hops must be cold treated before planting. Soak the seed in water until it is saturated and sinks to the bottom of the container, then chill it at temperatures of 35 to 40°F for a month to six weeks. Bring the seed indoors and plant in a flat or pot. Germination should be speedy and obvious. Seeds that are six months or more old may already have gone through the cold treatment and be ready to grow.

Hop pillows were once thought to cure insomnia and ease sleeplessness.

You may sow the hop seed in the garden or in a hop plot after the soil has warmed up. Gather the sprouts for a salad, and don't delay—hops can grow as much as 6 inches a day when things are going right. If the hop plants get away from you, console yourself with the thought that they make good animal fodder and will cover over any eyesore with a blanket of handsome leaves. A friend of mine grows hops up the telephone pole in his yard.

Hop seed is available from Thompson and Morgan and from J. L. Hudson.

Green Herb Mayonnaise

This is a rich and delicious dressing especially good with a variety of salad leaves.

> 2 teaspoons chopped chives
> 1 teaspoon chopped tarragon
> ½ teaspoon chopped chervil
> ½ teaspoon chopped dill
> 1 tablespoon chopped parsley
> 1 cup mayonnaise

Add the herbs listed above to the mayonnaise. Mix well and let stand for 15 minutes before serving. Vary the herbs to suit your taste and herb garden.

Yields 1 cup

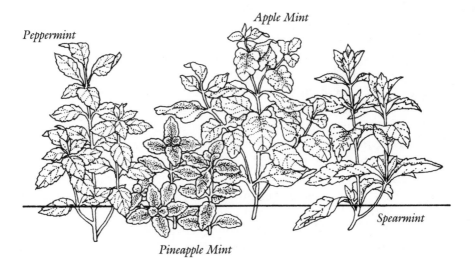

Peppermint

Apple Mint

Spearmint

Pineapple Mint

The Mints (*Mentha* spp.)

Walafrid Strabon, known also as Geoffroy the Cross-Eyed, was the medieval abbot of the German monastery Reichenau, and he wrote with only a little exaggeration that anyone wishing to name the different mints had to be one capable of counting all the sparks thrown out of Mount Etna in a volcanic eruption or all the fish that swam in the Red Sea. The species do hybridize easily, but although there are more than 600 named species, most experts feel these are variants or hybrids of 25 or so clearly identifiable species—aromatic, perennial herbs that originated in the temperate zone of the Old World.

Many of the cultivars have delightful flavors that make them of value in salads—apple mint, pineapple mint, bergamot mint, lemon mint, ginger mint, and others as well as the old standbys peppermint and spearmint.

It is a very pleasant hobby to collect different mint cultivars for a rich assortment of these refreshing plants, as long as one can cope with their heavy feeding habits and their weedy tendency to break out of bounds and multiply greatly.

All of the mints have menthol in tiny bumps along the stems and leaves that gives them the fresh, exhilarating character thought by the ancients to enliven a sluggish mind. Mint has been used for sore heads and against the bites of mad dogs and the stings of wasps and bees. Medieval women applied it vaginally in the belief it "hindreth conception," according to John Gerard.

Mint leaves, chopped or whole, can be added to green salads with very happy results. Look for new and different cultivars of mint in herb nurseries. The plant is a lusty grower and can be started directly in the bed or inside in flats, the seedlings to be transplanted outside after the frosts are over. Most of the mints are perennials in all but the northernmost parts of the country. They make fairly good windowsill plants, though they tend to be leggy. In the mint bed, plants gradually die out at the center and extend into new ground by way of creeping stolons. The heavy-feeding plants benefit from a shot of manure tea twice a month in the growing season, as well as side-dressings of compost and manure. Mint growers shift their plants every two years or so, setting the new, vigorous growth into fresh ground and discarding the old exhausted plants. The old mint beds should be planted to a green cover crop for soil restoration.

Catnip *(Nepeta cataria)*

Andre Simon has noted in *A Concise Encyclopedia of Gastronomy* that catnip has a minor place in the salad bowl. He remarks, "its very small young shoots are acceptable in small quantities in green salads . . . ," although the more mature leaves are much too pungent for culinary use.

Flat-Leaf Parsley

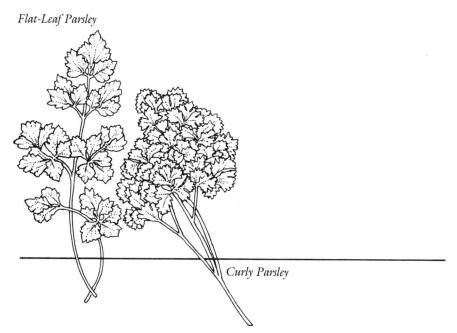

Curly Parsley

Parsley *(Petroselinum crispum)*

Nearly as useful in the kitchen as onions, excellent in a thousand dishes, a handsome garnish, a superb source of vitamins and minerals, parsley rarely gets into the American salad bowl, which is a great pity, for it adds fine color and texture, as well as a depth and richness of flavor no other salad green can rival. There are three species of parsley, but *Petroselinum crispum* and its variants *P. crispum* var. *neapolitanum* (Italian flat-leaved parsley) and *P. crispum* var. *tuberosum* (Hamburg or turnip-rooted parsley) are the ones of interest to the kitchen gardener.

Parsley is handsome as an edging or decorative border. Writes Rosalind Creasy, in her sensible volume, *The Complete Book of*

Edible Landscaping, on both the curly and flat-leaved parsleys:

> The dark-green of both these plants makes them usable as borders in herb or flower beds. Italian parsley, being taller, can also be grown in the middle of a flower border. I like to combine them in containers with orange violas and alpine strawberries.

Although parsley is a good addition to almost all salads, it is usually a minor player in salad drama. Only in the Middle East does it become a star. Tabbouleh is a wonderful hot-weather salad, available in premixed, dried form at specialty grocery stores, but it can be made fresh (and should be!) at home. It also calls for good quantities of mint, and the flavors can be varied subtly by using different kinds of mints.

Parsley and Bulgur Salad

    1 cup bulgur
    1 cup scallions
 1½ cups chopped fresh parsley
   ½ cup chopped fresh mint
    2 large ripe tomatoes cut small
   ½ cup fine olive oil
   ¼ cup fresh lemon juice
       lettuce leaves

Pour boiling water to cover over the cracked wheat. Let this stand for 30 minutes or until the water is absorbed and the wheat swells. Drain and press out any excess water with your hands.

Add the scallions, parsley, mint, and tomatoes. Mix all of the above ingredients with the oil and juice.

Arrange lettuce leaves on a platter and mound the mixture in the center. Surround the salad with more chunks of ripe tomatoes.

6 to 8 servings

VARIATION: Young leeks chopped fine can be substituted for scallions.

Parsley

A tremendous amount of folklore has gathered around parsley. It should never be given away by a gardener, says Margaret Baker in *Discovering the Folklore of Plants,* and she cites the case of a Welsh woman who gave parsley away and was crippled for life. There seems to be no danger if the person who wants the parsley simply helps himself. It was dangerous, too, to transplant parsley—a sure disaster in the family. The slow germination of parsley seed gave it the reputation of going down to the devil seven times before it sprouted. Evil-intentioned persons have only to pick a sprig of parsley and murmur an enemy's name to it, and the victim will fall dead within seven days. Nor must you gather parsley if you are in love, lest the beloved fade away and die. Finally, parsley was thought to have the power to weaken glass so much that a goblet rinsed in parsley water would shatter at a touch.

Parsley seed is very slow to germinate—it takes up to three weeks. Seeds should be soaked 24 hours before they are planted. You may start parsley indoors six to eight weeks before the last frosts. Parsley does not transplant very well from a flat of tangled-root seedlings, so take care to start the plants in their individual jiffy pots or cubes. The seed must be covered completely with soil for better germination. You can sow parsley seed directly in the garden.

Parsley prefers a rich, loamy soil in full sunlight, with several generous helpings of side-dressing during the season.

Neither seed nor started plants of parsley are difficult to find, but Nichols Garden Nursery in Oregon offers four or five cultivars—FOREST GREEN, a medium curly, slow-flowering parsley that is quite tender; SINGLE PARSLEY, a fine-flavored flat-leaf type; EXTRA CURLED DWARF, which makes a handsome garnish but is not a good salad parsley because of the rough texture of the very curly leaves; GIANT ITALIAN PARSLEY, which grows up to 3 feet tall and has a rich, full flavor and good texture making it one of the best salad parsleys.

VI
Oriental
Vegetables
in the Salad
Garden

We are increasingly fascinated by the oriental vegetables that have appeared in our produce markets and seed catalogs in the last few years. There are scores of curious fruits and exotic vegetables that cry out to be tried and grown fresh in a windowsill garden—gingerroot, bitter melon, bok choy, daikon, mitsuba.

In their native cusines, most of the oriental vegetables are cooked in some way—usually stir-fried or steamed—rather than eaten raw, an understandable procedure in countries where fields are fertilized with human manure. But westerners have discovered that some oriental vegetables grown in the home garden are excellent served raw in salads. A good many more are too tough or too strong in flavor to be really enjoyed in any way but cooked. Some of the stronger green leafy vegetables, such as bok choy, can be mollified by pouring boiling water over them and allowing them to stand for a few minutes. They are then drained and chilled before being chopped into the salad bowl as a minor ingredient.

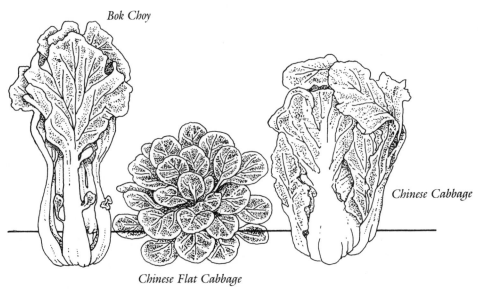

Bok Choy

Chinese Cabbage

Chinese Flat Cabbage

Chinese Cabbage *(Brassica pekinensis)*

There are three species of *Brassica* much grown in the orient that interest salad gardeners: the Chinese cabbage, bok choy, and Chinese flat cabbage. Chinese cabbage has been grown in China for at least 2,000 years. Its original habitat was the watery swamp, and it is a fast-growing plant that demands tremendous amounts of water (or so it seems to anyone who has to lug the waterbucket to the thirsty plants). An annual plant, it makes thick, sugarloaf heads. There are dozens of cultivars, ranging from petite little heads to behemoths of 15 or more pounds, and more cultivars appear in our seed catalogs every spring. The fleshy, tender, broad-ribbed leaves are mild, very crisp and juicy. Chinese cabbage can be profitably treated with a sesame oil and vinegar dressing piqued by crushed garlic and shredded scallions. This dressing poured over very thinly sliced Chinese cabbage and allowed to stand 10 minutes or so before serving makes a spicy and refreshing salad.

Chinese cabbage is a short-day, cool-weather plant that tends to bolt in midsummer heat. I grew wonderful big heads of it in a rainy mountain garden near the Canadian border some years ago. The rest of the vegetables were stunted with cold or half-drowned, but *Brassica pekinensis* made big, tight pale heads that gleamed like marble statues in the moonlight. Unless you have a similar climate, it is a good idea to start Chinese cabbage in midsummer like many chicories and endives, so that it can mature in the cool brief days of autumn. This tempered seasonal change gives the vegetable a very fine flavor and a texture of the highest quality.

Our choices among the Chinese cabbage cultivars increase every year. New seed imports from the orient and hybrids from breeders to suit specific climates or special markets give us Chinese cabbages that are slow to bolt in hot weather or resistant to many diseases. Today this excellent salad green can be grown nearly anywhere.

Vermont Bean Seed offers GREEN ROCKET, a popular, fast-growing hybrid that has replaced the familiar old MICHIHILI, once the only Chinese cabbage seed you could find. Green Rocket can reach an astounding 18 inches of height in 70 days and weigh as much as 5 pounds. SPRING A-1 matures at about the same time as ROCKET and has been bred for very early season planting so that the heads mature before the summer heat peaks. A slower-growing hybrid from Japan (90 days) is W-R SUPER HYBRID. This cultivar is disease resistant and should be planted in late summer for fall harvest. It is a good keeper and lasts for a long time in winter storage, where it remains firm and sound. Another late hybrid is WINTER QUEEN, which has an exceptionally thick and succulent midrib. Thompson and Morgan have NAGAOKA, also with a thick rib and tightly folded leaves that blanch the interior to a pale Nile green. Another, touted by Thompson and Morgan as a "new novelty" is TWO SEASONS, a slow-to-bolt type that can be planted in spring for summer harvest, or grown in summer for the autumnal cabbage rites. TREASURE ISLAND is a new introduction by Nichols Garden Nursery; this is a midwinter and early spring harvested plant grown only in milder climates where the plants can winter over. It makes big 6-pound heads. WONG BOK is sold by several seedsmen, including J. L. Hudson and Nichols; it is an old cultivar from China, short and stout (only 10 inches tall), and of excellent flavor and quality. However, it is susceptible to several brassica diseases and will bolt if planted in the spring. J. L. Hudson carries two very early Chinese cabbages—NOZAKI EARLY, a fat 5-pound head ready to be harvested in 60 days, and SOUTH CHINA EARLIEST, a very small 1-pound cabbagette that matures in a swift 45 days and should be sown in midsummer to mature in cool weather.

Chinese cabbage seedlings do not transplant well. It is best to sow them in place quite thinly. Thinning out a row of thickly seeded Chinese cabbage is hard on the little plants that are to stay—their roots are damaged and disturbed, and they often wilt away after such rough treatment. Handle with care.

Bok Choy (*Brassica chinensis* var. *chinensis*)

Bok choy has a thick, ivory white stalk and dark green leaves. (An unusual sort called Shanghai bok choy and much grown in Taiwan has a green stalk.) It is usually cooked in soups, side dishes, or stir-fried with beef, chicken or pork. However, the very young, most tender leaves and stalks make a nice addition to the mixed salad bowl. The best-quality bok choy is sown in summer and matured in fall. J. L. Hudson carries three cultivars, HIROSHIMANA, SANTO, and TAISAI, all Japanese types.

Bok choy is sown in late summer and allowed to develop in the cool autumn of fairly mild climates. I would grow it only as an incidental salad plant, choosing the youngest and most succulent stalks to add to other greens. The larger stalks should be stir-fried or added to Chinese soups. They are too tough for salad use. However, the stems may be steamed or stir-fried, chilled, and dressed with a vinaigrette or other dressing with good results.

Chinese Flat Cabbage *(Brassica chinensis* var. *rosularis)*

Chinese flat cabbage, which is sturdier than bok choy, can stand a little frost. It is a handsome plant that grows in a rosette flat against the ground, but the flavor is stronger than bok choy and the stalks are tougher. Only the very new plants can be used in salads, and even then it is definitely a matter of personal taste.

A solar growing frame is ideal for oriental vegetables and can provide you with a variety of salad ingredients throughout autumn and much of winter.

Solar Growing Frame

A solar growing frame is very much like a cold frame, although unlike a cold frame, it can be used to extend the growing season throughout the year in most areas—even when temperatures go below freezing. The north, east, and west walls of a solar growing frame, as well as the soil bed, are heavily insulated. The glazed side is oriented to the south, which allows the structure to collect solar heat during the day. At night an insulative shutter folds over the plants to keep the heat collected during the day inside the growing space. *Solar Growing Frame* (1980), edited by Ray Wolf, gives complete instructions for building this structure.

Researchers at the Rodale Research Center in Maxatawny, Pennsylvania, discovered that Chinese cabbages thrive in the damp, cool conditions and low light levels that prevail in a solar growing frame during the winter. A solar growing frame allows you to enjoy these tasty greens in the dead of winter when your only alternatives are to do without fresh greens or to buy ones that are less than fresh at your local grocery store.

Chinese Chives *(Allium tuberosum)*

We'll see these interesting members of the onion family later in the chapter on salad onions, listed as the garlic chive. Many seedsmen offer it as Chinese chives, its other common English name. The plant is used as a young, tender leaf in salads (the mature leaf is too tough), and the blossoms give a garlicky, rich flavor to any salad. In China the blossoms are thought to be too old to eat, and attention is lavished on the tight, cream-colored buds instead. These are the *gau choi fa* of Chinese markets, bundles of bright green stems like knitting needles (but tender!) headed with firm, creamy white buds. These can be minced and added to any salad.

There is yet another form in which these flavorful chives can be used—blanched to a tender, pale jonquil yellow. These are also sold in oriental markets and appear as thick bundles of limp yellow narrow ribbons. The flavor is quite pronounced, and the blanched chives are extremely tender. They have a very brief shelf life and are at their very best when freshly gathered. They can be blanched as endives are—by setting a dark pot or cover over the young plants for about ten days, or until they are blanched enough to suit the grower's taste.

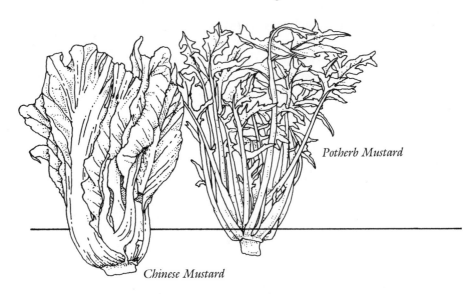

Potherb Mustard

Chinese Mustard

Chinese Mustard *(Brassica juncea)*

Here are half a dozen slightly different leaves known variously as bamboo mustard cabbage, Swatow mustard, sow cabbage, and the like, each cultivar having rather different taste characteristics and appearance. Bamboo mustard cabbage (*chuk gaai choi* in the marketplace) is very strong in flavor, hardly fit for the salad bowl (it looks like a young head lettuce thinned from a thickly sown row). Swatow mustard is the size and color of a head of lettuce, but the leaves are, so to speak, all stalk— thin, crisp, pale green, with just a frill of leaf at the ends. This is called *daai gaai choi* and is too pungent for eating raw. In China and Japan it is cured in brine to make a kind of oriental sauerkraut. It is too strong for salads. Sow cabbage is a tall celerylike creature with long tender stalks and a good amount of green leaf. It comes in a *rugosa* form with tough, reddish leaves, and in a foliar form, with mild and delicate green leaves rich in several vitamins. This one can be used for salads. Seed must be ordered from dealers of oriental seeds.

Geri Harrington, in her very useful book for gardeners, *Grow Your Own Chinese Vegetables* (1978), says this vegetable makes a good salad by itself when a vinaigrette dressing made with lemon instead of vinegar is used and several sliced, hard-cooked eggs are added in.

The mustard cabbages are cool-weather crops that are usually sown in late summer for maturation in the fall, or in fall for overwintering in mild climates. If you just want a few very young plants for the salad bowl, plant them any time, for you will use them young. There should be 4 inches between seedlings for the foliar types.

Potherb Mustard *(Brassica japonica)*

A very, very mild plant almost neutral in flavor, potherb mustard has a feathery pale green foliage that is quite beautiful in the salad bowl and as a garnish. The handsome appearance as well as its easy, tolerant growth, makes this a very useful plant in the salad garden. It is so unassertive in flavor that it can go into nearly every kind of salad. It is one of a handful of plants (like the Chinese cabbage) that enjoys a nasty, cold, and wet spring. It can be sown every ten days or so for successive crops.

C hinese parsley or coriander (Coriandrum sativum) *is one of our most ancient seasonings; it has been identified in an agricultural treatise of the fifth century in China and is known in oriental, Mexican, and Indian cuisines for its fragrant, distinctive flavor. The very young leaves may be used* sparingly *in salads.*

This pleasant plant is known in Japan as *mizuna*. The seed is planted up to half an inch deep, and the young plants thinned out to give at least a foot of space between seedlings. Rows are 18 to 20 inches apart. This is a thirsty plant, which needs plenty of water. It can be cut back after the first crop (it matures in 35 days) begins to go by, and a second crop will be forced. This practice is hard on the soil, so be sure to add compost liberally if you decided to practice cut-and-come-again techniques. Plan for a restorative cover crop later in the season.

Japanese Parsley (*Cryptotaenia japonica*)

Japanese parsley is called *mitsuba* on its home ground. It is similar to our wild honewort (*Cryptotaenia canadensis*) which is used in northern New England and Quebec as a potherb and soup flavoring. It has a strong, parsleylike flavor and should be used in moderation in salads. A little bit goes a long way. The advantage of having Japanese parsley in the garden is that it is very hardy and prefers the shade. This plant should be started in the garden in a moist shady section as early as possible in the first days of spring. It likes acid soil. Try it gingerly until you know if you like the flavor in your salad. Chopped hard-cooked egg is a good way to ameliorate strong tastes in salad greenery.

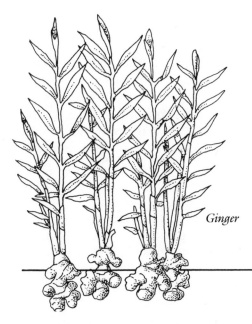

Ginger

Ginger (*Zingiber officinale*)

This is one of the most popular spices in the entire world down through the ages. There are about 85 subspecies that grow in tropical Asia and that are used for dyes, medicines, perfumes, condiments, and spices. The plant is propagated by division of the thick rhizomes or gingerroot. Some of the flowers of *Zingiber* species are exotically beautiful and fancied by collectors. A number of the edible oriental gingers have different flavors blending with the distinctive ginger taste—one is reminiscent of bergamot, and another has lemon overtones.

The gingerroot that we find in produce markets can be grown in pots at home to make a tall, red-stemmed plant with crisp, delicately flavored red stalks and showy flowers that are the ultimate in a spectacular salad. The stems may be cut up and tossed into a salad for an elusive fragrance and flavor.

Once in a while fresh gingerroot rhizomes are available from dealers in oriental seed, but gardeners who wish to grow the delicious plant in a pot can pore over the gingerroot bin at the supermarket looking for likely rhizomes.

Pick a firm, plump root that is neither spongy nor shriveled. If you look closely you may find several that are putting out shoots in the early spring. (Ginger is dormant in the winter.) Prepare a good big pot with a layer of gravel at the bottom for drainage, fill it with good rich potting soil, and plant the roots. Keep the soil moist and keep the pot in a warm but not sunny place. An hour or two of sunlight is all right but not more. Ginger grows in its natural habitat in the dappled shade of the tropical understory. Very gently, after about two weeks, scratch a little soil aside until the root is exposed. Check to see if shoots have appeared or if the rhizome has swollen to show they soon will emerge. If they are present, recover with earth and let them grow on. After the shoots are up and growing well, the plants can have more sunlight.

Ginger is a heavy feeder, so give it manure and compost teas. In a month or so you will have plenty of tender pink stems for salad use. If you wish, let the plants grow on for six or seven months or until they put up flower stalks. The beautiful and fragrant flowers, looking like tiny rare orchids, are stunning and delicious in a fruit or green salad.

Gardeners in warm climates will be able to grow ginger in the garden. Remember that in its natural habitat ginger is not only shielded from the direct rays of the sun, but it is rarely disturbed by wind. Keep it in a sheltered place if you grow ginger outdoors.

VII
The
Small
Onions

The *Allium* genus embraces **400** or more species of rhizomatous or bulbous plants with the distinct, rich onion odor. Some are grown for the flower border, some for the kitchen, and many grow wild. The culinary types are excellent creamed, in soups and sauces, on toast, in stuffings, and raw, boiled, fried, sautéed, baked, steamed, or prepared in a hundred other ways. They are used more than any other known plant in the world to flavor the foods of every cuisine. The salad gardener will find the small onions, as differentiated from the large-bulbed slicing onions, extraordinarily useful. They include shallots, chives, garlic, scallions, Welsh onions, Egyptian onions, and rocambole.

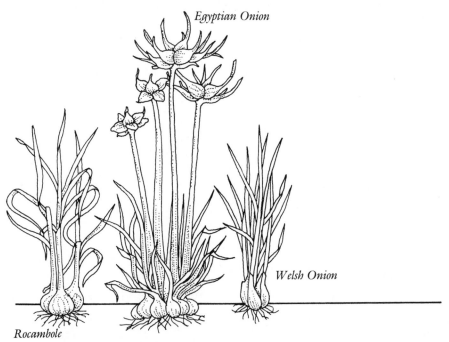

Egyptian Onion

Welsh Onion

Rocambole

Rocambole *(Allium sativum* var. *ophioscorodon)*

This is a handsome little perennial and because of its habit of curving its fruiting stems with the aromatic little purple bulbils on the end into sinous curves and circles, it is sometimes called serpent garlic. The tall, flat leaves are good chopped in salads, and the clusters of mild, garlic-tasting bulblets can be sliced into the salad or crushed into the dressing. The curious name is an anglicized form of the Danish word *rockenbolle*, or "onion of the rocks," for its habit of growing wild on stony soils.

The bulbils, which form on the top at the sources of new plants and when planted will themselves grow into an enlarged basal bulb, are similar to a leek. In two years each will be producing its own bulbils on the ends of sinuous scapes. Gertrude B. Foster and Rosemary F. Louden in *Park's Success with Herbs* describe the amusing habit of the plant:

> Before the clumps of flat, 18 inch long leaves begin to produce "flower" stalks, the plant is thick with greens, almost like garlic chives. Then from the middle of the clump rise round stems which make a complete circle before they reach their three foot height. The scapes unwind and hold their pointed buds high but at an angle that suggests a crane's bill. Finally, in midsummer the show ends with the splitting of the skin covering a cluster of popcorn kernel size, pleasantly garlic-tasting bulblets.

Rocambole can be grown in slightly shady areas and in nearly any type of soil. Seeds are available from Le Jardin du Gourmet, whose catalog says the seeds were "finally acquired . . . with great difficulty."

Egyptian Onion (*Allium cepa*, Proliferum Group)

My aunt Sarah Robinson gave me bulbs of this perennial (also called Egyptian tree onion) a few years ago. The tall hollow stems form greenish little bulblets clustered around the tip, and these enterprising little bodies send out roots while they are still up in the air. Usually the weight of the cluster of bulblets bends the cluster to the ground, and the little "onions" sink in their roots almost as you watch. This habit gives the plant the name of "walking onion," for in a few years an untended bed will walk its way across the garden. These hardy plants give you salad onions from the earliest spring until fall, for the ground bulbs may be used as well as the tip-growing bulbils.

Egyptian onions require almost no attention and grow nearly anywhere except in soil that is not well drained. These onions thrive in enriched soil, so to ensure juicy stalks, prepare the soil by adding compost or rotted manure. This self-propagating plant is immune to nearly all insects and diseases and is very easy to grow. Once established, a bed of Egyptian onions will grow forever, with harvesting being the easiest means of keeping the bed under control.

Thompson and Morgan's catalog confirms the above by describing Egyptian onions as "very hardy, very immune to onion fly, easy to grow and if not all the bulblets are harvested will continue to crop year after year." Le Jardin du Gourmet is another source for bulbs.

Welsh Onion (*Allium fistulosum*)

E. Lewis Sturtevant says Siberia is the origin of this very hardy, nonbulbed onion with the tender leaves. It gets it name, "Welsh" onion, from the German word *walsch* for "foreign." Some authorities think this is the ancestor of all onions. The new leaves that spring up from the swollen base of the stalks are tender and very nice chopped into a salad. The plants form their seeds in the second year and will self-seed or can be started in a separate bed. They like a rich soil and a generous amount of moisture. Dried-flower artist Sarah Milek, of Windsor, Vermont, gave me a clump of Welsh onions almost five years ago, but oddly enough they have never spread.

Welsh onions are also known as ciboule, multiplier onions, and Japanese bunching onions. The Urban Farmer offers two Japanese strains in its seed catalog—IWATSUKI, a fast grower that can be harvested 30 days after it is sown, and KUJOHOSO, a larger, slower-growing buncher.

Chive (*Allium schoenoprasum*)

Waverly Root, seeking to describe the flavor of chives, said in *Food*, "Suppose, in the symphony of tastes, you described the onion as the cornet: the chive would be the oboe." Highly individual, memorable, and beautiful are all adjectives that fit the chive. Most gardeners grow them for the mass of lavender globes that seem to hover over the slender stems, as much as for the fine, mild flavor.

Chive seed can be started indoors a month or so before the end of the frosts, then set into their permanent bed in the garden. Since it is an unnecessary chore to plant the little seedlings one by one, make the task easy by setting out small clumps of seedlings. Rich, improved soil and sunshine satisfy the chives. These plants are easy to grow and transplant, and most gardeners get a clump from a friend. Mine came from Helen Nichols of Heath, Massachusetts, some years ago, and the few plants I took from her vigorous thinning out of her wildflower beds where the chives had managed to get a foothold have increased to a long, thick row in my Vermont garden. I, in turn, have sent a dozen clumps out into the world to grow in the gardens of friends.

Too many gardeners go out to the chive bed with a big pair of shears and chop away until they have made a field of stubble in miniature—unsightly and unnecessary. Take a few minutes longer to cut chives. Cut off a few of the outer chives right at the base and distribute the cutting along the row; your gathering forays will be invisible.

The purple blossoms of chives can be picked and added to salads as a garnish or with other herb flowers. The delicate violet blue color mixed with pale yellow green lettuce cultivars is exquisite. The stems of chives themselves will become a striking jonquil yellow of the tenderest texture if they are blanched by growing them in the dark much as chicons are forced. They are quite fragile and easily broken grown this way but add lively color to salads.

Flowering Chinese Chive (*Allium ramosum*)

Another member of the *Allium* genus is the flowering Chinese chive, once named *A. odorum* and still listed that way in many catalogs. It is confused (just to make things interesting) with *A. tuberosum*, a similar chivelike allium described below. *A. ramosum* has thin, stiff round stems in a brilliant green color. On the ends of the slender little stalks are tight cream-colored buds. The taste is quite like scallions, and the tender stems are minced, flower buds and all, into a salad or used in stir-fried oriental dishes. Flowering chives are not quite as tender after the flower opens, and it is in the full bud stage that they are most esteemed by fanciers.

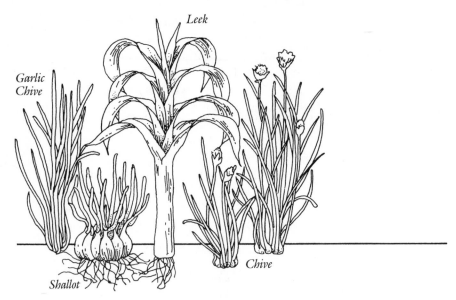

Leek

Garlic Chive

Shallot

Chive

Garlic Chive (*Allium tuberosum*)

Another hardy perennial, garlic chives has its own distinctive flavor. This allium has flat leaves, which are added to salads as are the sweetly fragrant starry flowers. The root is a rhizome, and the plants are divided by breaking the roots into sections.

A clump of the narrow flat leaves will grow up to 18 inches tall. The plants will seed themselves, and they grow well in pots. Some gardeners have planted them on banks where soil erosion is a problem, and the mass of white fluffy flower heads is striking. The flavor is definitely garlicky but far milder than biting into a clove of the real thing!

Shallot (*Allium cepa*, Appregatum Group)

Shallots used to carry the Latin name *Allium ascalonicum*, but they have been updated to the same name we use for onions with the aggregatum tag showing that these mild, sweet onions form bulb clusters like garlic. The flavor is the mildest of all the onion tribe, and in France, local cultivars of shallots are greatly esteemed in hundreds of dishes. In this country shallots are quite expensive and may only be found in gourmet food shops along with other such exotica as Witloof chicory, celeriac, and water-cress. It pays to grow shallots, and they winter over quite well, even in the North, if they are mulched. They're good keepers if cured in the sun as are onions before storing.

Shallot seed is rarely offered in our seed catalogs, and there is a belief that seed-sown shallots tend to bolt quickly to seed themselves. The delicious vegetable is sold in bulb form by the pound from many growers. Both the tops and the bulbs are used in salads.

Shallots have been known since earliest times. Pliny says the name comes from Ascalon, a town in Syria, and other later writers offer similar theories.

Leek (*Allium ampeloprasum*, Porrum Group)

Although the thick-stemmed leeks are usually put into cas-seroles and soups, they are also very good raw in salads when young. If you are thinning out a leek bed, put the extras into a salad.

Porrum was the Latin name for the leek, and the tasty onion has been known to mankind since the dimmest dark days of prehistory. In Pliny's day, the best leeks came from Egypt. Leeks attained a certain kind of fame from the habit of the notorious Nero who ate them for days at a time each month to clarify his voice, a practice that won him the not altogether complimentary nickname Porrophagus. Leeks, of course, are associated with the Welsh from their sixth century victory over the Saxons; in the battle the Welsh wore leeks as an identifying badge.

The French use leeks in hundreds of dishes, and the markets boast many regional cultivars, including GROS DU MIDI, LONG MEZIERES, the BIG ROUEN, the MONSTER OF CARENTEN, and the GIANT OF VERRIERES. All of these sound like acts in a sideshow, but shoppers new to the world of leeks will be staggered by the enormity of these vegetables.

The Swiss make an excellent salad by mixing butterhead lettuces and chopped leeks together, strewing crumbled bacon bits over the top, pouring a warm vinegar-bacon-dripping dressing over all, and serving the salad at once. (The bowl holding a bacon-dripping salad should always be prewarmed.)

Another European salad much relished by leek lovers involves cooking young leeks barely covered by salted water, then draining and chilling them for several hours. They are cut up and added to a green salad and dressed with a vinaigrette dressing.

August Leek Salad

    4 to 6 young leeks, cleaned and cut into ¼- to ½-inch pieces
    1½ cups cherry tomatoes, cut in halves
    1 teaspoon fresh tarragon leaves, chopped fine
    1 tablespoon sweet basil, chopped fine
    ½ cup Italian or French dressing
    2 heads bibb or other tender lettuce, washed and dried
    ¼ cup garlic croutons

Gently mix the leeks, tomatoes, herbs, and dressing in a bowl. Let this mixture stand while arranging a shallow salad bowl with the lettuce. At the last minute mix the croutons into the leek mixture, heap the salad on the lettuce, and serve at once.

8 servings

Slicing Onions (*Allium cepa*)

Mature onions may be too pungent in taste (except for the mild "salad" types) to use raw in the salad bowl. The pungency can be softened by slicing a strong onion very thinly, laying the slices in a bowl, and pouring boiling water to cover over them. Allow them to stand 4 or 5 minutes, then drain, and add to the salad. Chilling restores some of the crispness but not much.

Spanish salads often use mild raw Bermuda onions sliced thin. Unusual and very good is a bowl of mixed torn lettuce leaves, three oranges peeled, seeded and sliced, and one mild onion peeled and sliced paper-thin. These are all tossed together and dressed with a slightly sweetened vinaigrette mixture.

Scallions are nothing more than young onions before they have made a bulb of any size. Many gardeners like to grow a crowded row of greentails as they are often called, just to use in salads. The taste can be quite pungent.

Onions and garlic can add a special zip to salads and other dishes. Slicing onions come in a variety of shapes and sizes, from the large, mild Bermudas to smaller, more cylindrical torpedo types. Onions that are too pungent to eat raw can be sliced very thin and soaked in boiling water to tone down their flavor. And storage can become decorative by braiding together the tops of onions and garlic bulbs and hanging the braids in the kitchen until you are ready to use them.

Garlic (*Allium sativum*)

There is no median position on garlic; one likes it and eats it heartily, or one detests it and shuns it assiduously. Crushed garlic plays a leading role in many classic salad dressings, but rarely do the pungent cloves enter the salad bowl in a larger size.

Few people indulge in cloves of raw garlic, though E. Lewis Sturtevant remarks "In many parts of Europe, the peasantry eat their brown bread with slices of garlic which imparts a flavor agreeable to them." We read that the Romans included it as a vital part of a laborer's or soldier's diet, for it was believed to give the eater strength. The bite and strength of the bulbs inevitably made garlic part of the medieval pharmacopoeia, and it was thought to mitigate the effects of mad dog bites, to clear stagnant, fetid water, to soften the disastrous consequences of certain poisonous plants taken in, and to kill worms in children. Colonial livestock was dosed with garlic, and even chickens seemed to brighten up when fed chopped garlic. Some of the medical claims for garlic have been revived in recent years.

Usually salad makers use garlic cloves to rub the vivid perfume into the bowl, enough to flavor a salad subtly. A small crushed clove in the dressing can perk it up tremendously. But John Evelyn, who balked at very little for his salads, recoiled in horror from the idea of garlic corrupting the gentler flavors. He wrote in *Acetaria*:

> Garlick, Allium; dry towards Excess; and tho by both Spaniards and Italians and ther more Southern People familarly eaten with almost everything, and esteemed of such singular Vertue to help Concoction, and thought a Charm against all Infection and Poyson . . . we yet think it more proper for our Northern Rustics, especially living in Uliginous and moist places, or such as use the Sea; Whilst we absolutely forbid it entrance into our Salleting, by reason of its intolerable Rankness, and which made it so detested of old that the eating of it was . . . part of the Punishment for such as had committed the horrid'st Crimes.

Garlic, like shallots, is rarely grown from seed, but from cloves sold by the pound and set out early in the spring. The bed or row must be kept weed-free and well watered. By late summer the bulbs will be fat and plump, and are ready for harvest when the leaves begin to yellow and fall over. They should be sun-cured for several days before storage.

One of the most handsome harvests for kitchens are garlic bulbs in a braid, which bring a high price in specialty markets. The leaves are allowed to dry and wither in the sun, and are tightly braided into a thick rope with the bulb clusters forced to the front of the braid. Many gardeners grow enough garlic to make extra ropes for sale at nearby farmers' markets for some healthy garden income or as harvest presents for friends who did not plant their own.

Dropping garlic cloves into a mole tunnel was supposed to send the occupant hurtling from his suddenly high-flavored home. Bulb growers might want to test this attractive theory.

Garlic likes a rich, moist soil. It is available from many sources. Elephant garlic is a fairly recent introduction, and it is a mild, very large bulb that can weigh up to 1 pound. This gentle garlic was introduced by the Nichols Garden Nursery in Oregon two decades ago, and it has become very popular in California where it is grown commercially. Several seed and nursery suppliers, as well as Nichols, offer elephant garlic. Nichols also offers top-setting garlic, which, like the Egyptian onion, produces bulblets at the top of the plant. The flavor is pronounced.

There are many, many other small onions. Salad gardeners may like to try new ones that swim into their ken. They are all handsome, valuable plants, and John Evelyn might have changed his mind on those of strong flavors for the salad bowl if he had only owned a garlic crusher.

VIII

Other
Salad
Furniture

*A*lmost anything that grows, from gooseberries to walnuts, dandelions to dates, and asparagus to yams, can be used in salads. In this book I have tried to explore the delights of the green, leafy herbs and salad plants that make up the classic tossed salad, a piquant mélange of leaf, bud, and flower that changes as the seasons advance. Connoisseurs of the green salad eschew the current fad of adding sliced raw mushrooms, cooked asparagus tips, artichoke hearts, or even tomato or cucumber slices.

Yet there is a school of admiration for the more robust salads that include more tangible and corporeal fruits of the garden than the ephemeral but sprightly leaves and stalks. Indeed, the hearty dish called Chef's Salad includes hard-cooked eggs, capers, and slices of ham, turkey, and cheese. In such a salad, these additions seem to be the focus of the chef, and the true salad part—the green leaves and stalks and herbs—are usually represented by watery chunks of commercial head lettuce that add little to the dish except architectural support for the heavy strips of meat and cheese. The Chef's Salad bears little resemblance to the light but rich and spicy rocket salad of early spring, or the small salads of great variety containing as many as 15 or 20 kinds of tender lettuce and herb leaves, or the buttery, nutty savor of a salad of forced chicons, or the salads with great character featuring the chicories and endives. But there are salads of merit that use a larger palette of flavor and texture than just stalk and leaf.

Beets, celery, radishes, tomatoes, bell peppers, cucumbers, hearts of palm, and avocado—whatever is local, garden fresh and good—can be good and pleasant additions to the salad if used in moderation and balanced against the basic foundation of mixed greenery.

There are several things to avoid in making and growing these fuller-bodied salads. The mixture and balance of the green salad leaves that support the character of the salad should be as extensive and varied as though no coarser materials were being used; and the additions to the salad should be moderate and delicately cut to avoid at all costs the effect of large lumps of vegetables dominating the thin, fine herbs and lettuces. Tomatoes to be added to green salads should be carefully chosen and be either the meaty, low-pulp salad tomato types or tiny cherry, husk, or currant tomatoes used whole. Cucumbers in salads should be used young when the seeds are so tender that they are almost invisible, and they should always be sliced very thin. Very juicy cucumbers may be sliced, weighted with a plate, and chilled several hours in the refrigerator before they are drained and added to the salad.

Everyone is familiar with the soggy salad, a mass of washed lettuce leaves and wedges of big juicy tomatoes and thick wet rounds of cucumber. The dressing is added, the salad is mixed, and the diners helped to dripping, saturated forkfuls of salad so wet with vegetable juices that the lettuce leaves cling together and as much as half a cupful of mingled liquids pool in the bottom of the bowl. If you grow only the juicy, pulpy kinds of tomatoes, scoop out the pulp and put it aside for cooking, and then cut the fleshy walls into salad-size pieces.

Most of the cherry tomatoes are still quite large to be used whole in salads, for they give a strong, almost overpowering burst of juice and flavor in the mouthful of salad, but this is still preferable to the wet salad soup that comes from slicing them. The very tiny currant tomatoes—RED CURRANT and YELLOW CURRANT—are excellent in green salads. They are old cultivars and hard to find. Also suitable in size and delicacy is the sweet piquancy of ripe husk tomatoes, little yellow globes the size of marbles and very fine in the premier mixed green salad.

Radishes call for a little care, too. These crisp roots come in a great variety of colors, flavors, and sizes. To grow a tender, sweet-fleshed, solid radish is a task more difficult than many gardeners realize, but if you do, the result makes an excellent salad addition. Radish slices tend to cling to the sides of a glass salad bowl like limpets to the rocks but stay distributed through the mixture in a wooden bowl.

Marmande Tomato

Cherry Tomato

Currant Tomato

Tomatoes *(Lycopersicon lycopersicum)*

The insipid, mealy, tasteless tomatoes sold in the supermarket have received so much bad press it's a wonder growers still bother with them. The tough, square "red rocks" as they are called in the green grocery trade, ship very well, hang around on the shelf for weeks without noticeable deterioration (critics say that a fruit so poor in quality has nowhere to go but up), and people still buy them, probably more for salad imagery and tradition than anything else.

But millions of triumphant gardeners, if they grow nothing else, try for the reddest, tastiest, meatiest tomatoes they can get. The tomato is the number one choice of home gardeners. A growing group of collectors of old-time tomatoes concentrates on cultivars like TROPHY, LONG TOM, COOK'S FAVORITE, GOLDEN SUNRAY, and other darlings of the nineteenth century almost lost to modern gardeners. New specialty seed houses and the efforts of Kent Whealy's Seed Savers organization have brought many of the old kinds back into circulation. One of the beauties of the old tomato cultivars is that they are open-pollinated types and you can save the seed.

Some of the tomatoes listed here are too juicy to be added to green salads but make a delicious salad by themselves. An example is a ripe, sun-warmed MARMANDE, an old French cultivar of flat, lumpy shape but incomparable flavor. The Marmande

to find, though delicious, prolific, and tiny. Regional seed exchange groups are a possible source of currant tomato seed. Joy Larkcom's fine book, *The Salad Garden*, gives hope that gardeners are still interested in growing these good little tomatoes, so excellent in the salad bowl.

Salade de Tomates

The standard French treatment for full-bodied, ripe tomatoes of good flavor was to scald them for 30 seconds in boiling water, then peel them, cut off the tops, and remove the se~~ and pulp. The pulp was set aside for cooking uses ~~ tomato jam.

The tomatoes were then sliced, n~~ a clean, four-fold cloth, and a~~

Just before servin~~ ~~ slices were arranged on a platter and seas~~ ~~, vinegar, ground pepper, and chopped parsle~ ~~soning was varied with finely chopped fresh ~~ ~~ves, fennel, tarragon, and basil, each imparting ~~ive taste to the dish.

Saving the Seed of Open-Pollinated Tomatoes

Better and quicker germination is only one of the side benefits of saving your own tomato seed. (Naturally one doesn't save the seed of hybrid plants, since Mendelian laws dictate that only a few plants will be like the hybrid you grew the season before, and most of the offspring will be throwbacks to earlier ancestors.) But open-pollinated tomatoes breed true, and the flowers are usually pollinated before they are fully open. Nevertheless, to prevent any possible cross-pollination and to keep your cultivars true, a distance of at least 25 feet should separate different tomato cultivars.

The selection of plants begins early. Watch the plants for valuable characteristics such as strength and sturdiness, early blossoming, abundance of fruit, and finally, flavor, and time of maturity. Naturally, you would not select a tomato with disease or malformed shape unless the fruits were of incomparable flavor and unobtainable in any other way.

Mark the likely plants early on with colored tape (loggers' and surveyors' tape in gaudy-colored plastic is cheap and good) or tagged garden stakes. Keep your eye on your chosen plants, and if troubles develop, remove the marker and strike the plants from your seed list. Keep only the best.

Tradition holds that the best tomato seed comes from the four tomatoes on the third or fourth truss, the fruits that are closest to the main stem. Others think that the best tomatoes for seed are the first set of fruits in the second truss.

Allow the chosen fruits to ripen, and pick them when they are very ripe and soft, but not rotten. Lay them in a clean plastic flat and allow them to mellow to the point of pulpy softness but not to the point of decay.

Have a clean bucket of water ready. Pierce the tomatoes with the point of a sharp knife and dump the pulp and seeds into the bucket of water. (Use a jar if you are doing only a few tomatoes.) Let the bucket or jar stand three to four days while the mixture ferments. The temperature should hold at about 65°F. If you have a cold snap and the water is chilled, give it another day or so; if there is a heat wave, fermentation may be in good process after 24 to 36 hours.

As the mixture ferments defective seed and the pulp will float to the top of the bucket after a few days of fermentation, and the good seed will lie at the bottom. Skim off the detritus and drain the water away from the good seeds. Rinse the seeds gently in clear water and drain again.

Spread the seed out on nylon screening to dry. Stir it occasionally to keep the seeds from clumping together. When the seeds are dry, put them in a bowl and mix in some fine dry sand. Rub the seeds gently between your palms; the sand will give them a smooth, clean surface that lessens the chance of mold. Finally, shake the seed in a coarse mesh sieve to get rid of the sand, and store the clean dry seed in an airtight container away from the light. Be sure the container is accurately labeled, such as "Uncle Joe's Moonlight Wonder/Sept. 1985."

Tomato seed will stay viable for about four years. Three pounds of tomatoes can give you as many as 1,500 healthy, good seeds. With careful selection you can improve the quality of your tomatoes each year, until you grow fruit money cannot buy. It is possible for an attentive gardener to develop a unique, thick-meated, low-juice tomato ideal for the salad bowl, all in the backyard garden.

Black Spanish Radish

China Rose Radish

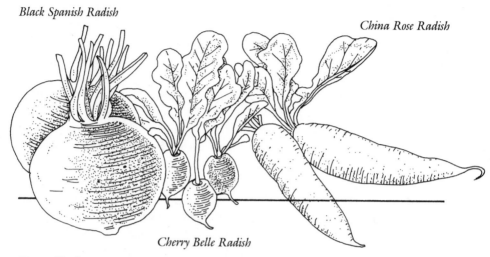

Cherry Belle Radish

Radishes *(Raphanus sativus)*

A crisp, firm, tender radish of good flavor and a slight nip is hard to find in our gardens. Radishes are an early, cool-weather crop that grows rapidly and matures in a few weeks. They dislike crowding. If they are planted in the late spring or summer, they must have firm, cool, moist soil or they will be stringy, tough, and unpleasantly acrid in taste. But if they are quickly grown in cool temperatures, the radish, in its great variety of colors and shapes, adds brightness and crisp texture to a green salad. Large mild radishes, chilled and sliced very thin, make a good salad when mixed with the tender bibb or Boston lettuces, and brightened by finely cut herbs and small onions.

The ancient Greeks held radishes in such esteem, that in offerings to Apollo, facsimiles of turnips were brought forth made out of lead; beets were fashioned from silver; but radishes, greatly esteemed, were given to the god beaten out of pure gold.

Even in ancient times radishes were known in many shapes and forms—long, round, red, white, black, purple-tinged, three-colored. By the time John Gerard was writing *Herbal*, he could list many radishes of all sorts, and, after noting the several medicinal qualities and uses of the pungent roots, remarked that radishes were often eaten "with bread in stead of other food." John Evelyn, our hero of the salad bowl, preferred the young seedling leaves to the roots in his salad, and remarked in *Acetaria*: "Radish, *Raphanus*, albeit rather medicinal than so commendably accompanying our Sallets (wherein they often slice the larger Roots) are much inferior to the young Seedling leaves and Roots, raised on the Monthly Hotbed almost the whole year round." This is a very good salad use of radishes almost unknown in our kitchens.

Batty Langley, whose important *New Principles of Gardening* was published in 1728, had much to say about the radish, all of it interesting. "The Root is of a taper Form, running down about six or eight inches, with divers small Fibres breaking from its Sides: The top part of the Root is of a very dark or blackish red, its middle part of a beautiful red, and the lower part quite white; as also are the inward Parts in general, and of a sharp or mordicant Taste." He goes on to comment that if radishes are eaten before dinner, they "are troublesome to the Stomach, and cause much Belching." But when either the leaves or roots are eaten raw in salads, they "procure a good Appetite, provoke Urine, dissolve clustered Sand, and expel it."

In Langley's day, radish seed was thickly sown, as if it were cress, and the seedlings cut off for salad use the way John Evelyn preferred them. These little leaves were mixed into salads of "small Herbs," about three times as many radish leaves as the rest of the ingredients.

Langley mentions a radish-growing trick I have not seen mentioned elsewhere:

> To have Radishes early in the Spring, at the end of *August*, or beginning of *September*, sow some Seed under a warm Wall, or rather on a decay'd Hot-Bed, that during the time of Frosts, Snow, &c. they may be preserved therefrom; and about the middle of *February*, or sooner, they will be fit for the Table. And that these may be succeeded by a second Crop, at the end of *September*, or rather a little sooner, sow some Seed in the border of a *South* Wall, that they may get above Ground in their SeedLeaf, before their growth is stopt by the Winter's Cold; and if they are preserved from very great Frosts and Snow in the Winter, they will be in Season about the middle of March.

The radish came early to this country, and by 1806 Bernard M'Mahon names ten cultivars in *Gardener's Calendar*. Late in the century Vilmorin-Andrieux spouts out a flood of cultivar names, ROUND, SCARLET FRENCH, EARLY SCARLET, EARLY WHITE-TIPPED SCARLET, DEEP SCARLET, SMALL EARLY WHITE, WHITE-TIPPED PURPLE, SMALL EARLY YELLOW, and then goes on to name seven olive-shaped cultivars including the famous FRENCH BREAKFAST radish, a bright pink, blunt radish with a pure white tip. He proceeds then at a leisurely pace toward the long radishes, and names eight, the most striking, the MAN'S CORKSCREW RADISH, "An exceedingly distinct variety." He describes it: "About one-fourth . . . of the root protrudes overground, and that part is of a dull white colour, more or less tinged with pale green. The underground portion is pure white, seldom straight, but most usually twisted in a zigzag manner, like a corkscrew, in consequence of which the root can rarely be pulled up without breaking off and leaving a part behind in the ground." Still his radish list is not exhausted. He goes on to the summer and autumn radishes—six of them—and then tackles the winter radishes, seven great monsters, before he throws in the final five "other varieties." The rat-tailed radish earns a separate section.

Today's radish fancier would have to dig deep and hard into the catalogs to come up with half the cultivars Vilmorin names. But the search for a broad spectrum of radish types is worthwhile, for the salad bowl is enhanced with slivers, slices, and rosettes of radish. One orders a radish here, a radish there, and builds up a fine collection.

Growing Radishes

Radishes do well interplanted with lettuce, which shades the soil and keeps it a bit cooler. A light mulch of compost or old hay aids radish growth late in the season by cooling the soil and holding in needed moisture.

Root maggots are sometimes a problem with radish crops. Some gardeners swear by wood ashes to prevent these pests. A good crop rotation schedule that keeps radishes out of soil inhabited by members of the Cruciferae family the year before is the best preventative measure.

Occasionally "keeper" radishes can be found—those that will endure winter storage in a root cellar and can be enjoyed all winter long though they begin to shrivel as the days lengthen. Keeper radishes are generally sown in midsummer for fall harvest and storage in the damp sand of the root cellar. If planted in the spring they will bolt, and their roots will be tough, hot, and hollow. Vermont Bean Seed offers three keepers: CHINA ROSE (cultivated before 1885), BLACK SPANISH LONG (one from Vilmorin-Andrieux's list), and a Japanese hybrid, TAMA, a huge, white, perfectly cylindrical root up to 18 inches long. Redwood City Seed tops this in its list of six Japanese winter radishes by including the SAKURAJIMA MAMMOTH, a monster that grows to more than a foot in diameter and weighs up to 50 pounds. Some radish! These big winter radishes are usually cooked or pickled or fed to livestock and do not make very good salad fare unless one is desperate.

Radish Seedpods in Salads

A curious and delicious addition to the salad bowl comes from the late Andre Simon who wrote in the *Vegetable* volume of *A Concise Encyclopedia of Gastronomy*:

> Amateur gardeners do not trouble to let their radishes run to seed for the sake of saving the seed, but it does happen that a few radishes are not pulled in time and do run to seed. If the little pods are picked when just formed, when the little seeds inside are still minute, these seed-pods can be added to any green salad; they are tender and their slightly peppery taste is quite pleasant, as well as likely to be quite new to most of one's friends.

The small salad radishes are occasionally cooked and served with butter or sauces, but I agree with Andre Simon, who writes in *A Concise Encyclopedia of Gastronomy*, "Radishes, like grapefruit, can be and have been cooked, but they are not meant to be and the practice is not to be encouraged."

Salad radishes such as EARLY SCARLET GLOBE, SPARKLER WHITE TIPPED, FRENCH GOLDEN, CHERRY BELLE, French Breakfast, and HAILSTONE are all good starters for the radish garden. French Golden is an outstanding salad radish, a lovely radiant yellow that enhances the yellow green butterhead lettuces. The whole salad bowl seems to have a golden glow when a few tablespoons of blanched chives or the buds of Flowering Chinese Chives are added. Nichols Garden Nursery carries French Golden and French Breakfast, SPARKLER, ICICLE, Hailstone and Cherry Belle, and offers a sampler containing all but the Golden.

The rat-tail radish *(Raphanus caudatus)* is an engaging and ornamental plant to grow. The root is not edible, a stringy, narrow thing, but the plant puts forth enormously long, curled, slender siliques up to 18 inches in length and the thickness of a narrow pencil. These mild, very good "pods" can be cut into salads, or lightly stir-fried after cutting them into bite-size pieces, and then mixed into other salad ingredients. The taste is delicate and pleasant, unlike anything but itself. Seed for this special plant is available from Greenleaf Seeds.

Bell or Sweet Peppers (*Capsicum annuum*, Grossum Group)

The bell pepper is one of the most beautiful vegetables on the face of the earth. Its deep green patent-leather gleam, its fine shape, sometimes curved and set in shadowed folds, and the largeness of the fruits, are all highly satisfying to the gardener and salad maker.

This interesting plant has its origins in tropical America, and it is quite tender to frost. These peppers are the mildest and sweetest in a family of about 20 species that break down into hundreds of cultivars and strains in a bewildering range of colors, sizes, shapes, and pungencies. There are 201 pepper cultivars stored in the National Seed Storage Laboratory in Virginia. The fiery, hot, and tiny bird's-eye peppers, the mild but brilliantly colored paprika peppers, the huge Big Jim bred by New Mexico's famous "Mr. Chili," Roy Nakayama, are all related. The chilies are the source of one of the world's most popular spices, used in the cuisines of many countries, from India to the orient, from Mexico to South America.

Bell peppers and the chilies are both grown as annuals, although in the right climate most of them are perennials. I had a gardener friend who lifted a prize pepper plant from his garden at the end of the season and kept it as a houseplant for four years before it succumbed to the unwelcome attentions of a cat. I have tried several times to duplicate his feat, but the transplant shock to these full-grown plants has always been too severe. Patio gardeners might like to try growing a pepper plant in a 5-gallon container.

There are many accounts of explorers and European adventurers' first contact with the fiery chilies, from Columbus onward, but the sweet pepper is not often mentioned. Sturtevant mentions Lionel Wafer's 1699 *Voyage and Description of the Isthmus of America*, where was written "They have two sorts of pepper,"—the natives of the Isthmus—"the one called Bell-pepper, the other Bird-pepper, each sort growing on a weed or shrubby bush about a yard high. The Bird-pepper has the smaller leaf and is most esteemed by the Indians."

It was also the chili that became the rage of Europeans, much grown in physic gardens for the wonderful medicinal properties ascribed to it. The sweet pepper was fairly ignored except in the gardens and kitchens of Spain and Italy. But in the great gastronomical surge of interest in all things edible in the eighteenth and nineteenth centuries, chefs discovered the bell pepper was exceedingly useful in sauces, and it could be stuffed with a marvelous variety of foods, including left-overs. The bell pepper had arrived.

Vilmorin-Andrieux remarks on the sweet peppers:

> The pods of some of the large kinds, which are very fleshy and not hot to the taste, are used as vegetables. A good instance of the slowness with which the use of vegetables is made known is afforded by the large green mild variety of *Capsicum*, which is so much eaten over a large part of Spain and some of the adjoining French departments. It was carried by the Spaniards into Naples during their dominion there in the sixteenth and seventeenth centuries, and has ever since remained in common use there, without spreading farther. It makes an excellent salad, having all the flavour of the *Capsicum* without pungency, and enters into various light and pleasant dishes of the Italian and Spanish cooks.

The sweet pepper was not an uncommon vegetable in American gardens, and Bernard M'Mahon listed, in 1806, the LARGE

HEART-SHAPED PEPPER, CHERRY, BELL, and LONG-PODDED as familiars. Late in the century, Vilmorin lists LARGE BELL, BULL-NOSE or SWEET MOUNTAIN PEPPER, MONSTROUS (also called SHEEP'S HEAD by some), SPANISH MAMMOTH, and AMERICAN BONNET, the last a sweet red pepper. Sturtevant adds several popular American varieties to Vilmorin's list—GIANT EMPEROR and GOLDEN DAWN.

Today sweet peppers come in red, yellow, and green. There are hybrids, old cultivars, early fruits, and big fruits. Some are shaped like bananas. Others are bred for good drying character-istics (the MILD CALIFORNIA PAPRIKA pepper from Vermont Bean Seed is one such). Gardeners can choose almost anything they want in the sweet pepper line except stripes. Seed saver exchanges are a source of old cultivars no longer commercially available.

An absorbing hobby is collecting the seeds of old vegetable varieties and growing them in the home garden. And peppers have lured many collectors to them by their diversity and beauty as well as utility. Carolyn Jabs' *The Heirloom Gardener* (1984) uses illustrations in the margins of several old cultivars from seed catalogs of yesteryear, and several are peppers. Of interest is LARGE SQUASH PEPPER, a very large and thick-fleshed fruit with curious ridges like a squash or pumpkin. This was once carried by Ferry Seeds and described as "flesh mild, and pleasant to the taste, although possessing more pungency than many other sorts. . . ."

Peppers are started inside in the North, as every gardener knows who lives there. The seedlings can be transplanted to the garden only when all danger of frost is past. Peppers must not be stressed by any lack of water, particularly during blossom and fruit-set stages of their growth. Neither can they stand poor drainage nor waterlogged conditions. When harvesting peppers, it is better to cut the fruits off than to twist or pluck them. By picking the peppers as they swell and ripen, harvest can be stretched over many weeks, for the obliging plants will strain to produce the utmost fruits.

Sweet peppers can be added with profit to nearly every salad when sliced into very thin strips. A large salad is beautifully decorated with thin rings of sweet pepper and mild onion ar-ranged over the top. Seasonal edible flowers worked into designs with the pepper rings can make a centerpiece salad for a buffet.

A sweet pepper salad *a la créole* is given in the *Larouse Gas-tronomique*. Sweet peppers, either red or green, are blanched in boiling water, seeded, and peeled. They are sliced into the sizes and shapes desired and arranged in separate mounds on salad plates. Beside the peppers are heaped spoonfuls of cooked, cooled rice. The mounds of rice are crowned with slices of ripe tomato, and a teaspoon of chopped chives is sprinkled over the rice and the peppers. The dressing is vinaigrette piqued with paprika, and just before the salads are served, the dressing is labeled over both rice and peppers.

Carol Truax, in her useful book *The Art of Salad Making* (1968), gives a Russian sweet pepper salad, *Sladky Perezs*. Here, sweet peppers are cut into quarters and blanched in boiling water until tender, then drained, peeled, and chilled. A mustard dressing is poured over the peppers, and the salad is allowed to stand several hours in the refrigerator (or out on the steppes) before serving.

It's odd how many green pepper salad recipes direct that the peppers be blanched or half-cooked first; raw green pepper salads are very good, are rich in vitamins, and have an agreeably crunchy, juicy texture that is superior to the limp flesh that comes after blanching. Peppers are splendid when cut julienne and added to a classic Witloof salad. They can be cut in thin rings and mixed with rings of very mild onion and celeriac julienne, all dressed with an herb vinaigrette or cream dressing.

Cucumbers *(Cucumis sativus)*

The cucumber, a tender annual, is frost damaged very easily and doesn't transplant terribly well. Beetles and other insects, diseases such as mosaic virus and scab all prey on the cucumber. Yet home gardeners without cucumbers in the plot are rare—it is a favorite vegetable in this country for salads, pickles, and crudités. The cucumber is glorious in all sorts of cucumber salads and prized for its refreshing cool taste. It is synonymous with the heat of high summer and the drone of cicadas. What could be more pleasant and cooling than to sit in the shady summer house eating cucumber salad?

The cucumber's origins lie in south Asia, and it has been cultivated by humans since ancient times, for at least 3,000 years. It was known in ancient China, in Egypt and Greece, and by the time of the Romans, hothouse cucumbers were forced out of season for the gourmet trade. The Emperor Tiberius insisted on cucumbers for his table every day of the year, and centuries later cucumbers were still high on the list of royal desiderata, for Charlemagne ordered cucumbers planted on his estates.

In England the cucumber was apparently grown in the fourteenth century, then lost through neglect in periods of war and pestilence. It was reintroduced in 1573, and by 1629 John Parkinson wrote, "in many countries they use to eat coccumbers as wee doe apples or Peares." Sturtevant noted cucumbers were still eaten as hand fruits in Russia and Japan in the late nineteenth century.

The long green vegetables were often called "cowcumbers" in earlier centuries, but Nicholas Culpeper remarks waspishly that this is the pronunciation of the vulgar. John Evelyn, of course, has something to say of the cucumber: he praises it as making

Too Few Is Better Than Too Many

Batty Langley wrote a good deal on cucumbers and their culture in his 1728 *New Principles of Gardening* and named ten cultivars known in his day. He was, however, a little uneasy about overindulgence in the vegetable:

> When Cucumbers are very young and picked, 'tis usual to eat the outside Rind of the Fruit with them; but when they are largely grown, as fit for slicing, to be either fried, stew'd or eaten raw, they are generally pared, and then used. 'Tis a very great Custom amongst a great many People to make choice of the very largest Cucumbers, believing them to be the best, which are not, but instead thereof, are the very worst, except such as are quite yellow. Therefore in the Choice of Cucumbers, I recommend those that are about three Parts grown, or hardly so much, before those very large ones, whose Seed are generally large, and not fit to be eaten, excepting by such Persons whose stomachs are very hot. . . . But herein observe, that 'tis better to eat too few, than too many; and if your Stomach will bear, to eat a good many Onions sliced amongst them, 'tis much better than to eat them alone.

an outstanding salad by itself vinaigrette or perked up with cloves and onion!

As for the kinds of cucumbers through the ages, they were legion: round, long, smooth skinned, netted like melons, prickly, monstrous in size, or itty-bitty pickling cucumbers. The Vilmorin-Andrieux list includes nearly 30 cultivars, some the small Russian types such as the BROWN NETTED OF KHIVA. E. Lewis Sturtevant divided the cucumbers into six groups, "many kinds . . . extraordinarily distinct." He lists a number of old commercial American cultivars and a French type, the BONNEUIL LARGE WHITE, which was grown in the environs of Paris for use in perfumes.

Today, gardeners choose not only among the various cultivars for the kinds of cucumbers they wish to grow, but among cultivars with multiple disease resistance bred in. Nor are we restricted to monoecious cucumbers (male and female flowers on the same plant), but we can buy the seed of gynoecious (all female flowers) cucumbers that yield tremendously heavy crops. Many of the new pickling cultivars are gynoecious, but the crop production, while heavy, tends also to be short. This is fine for a mad burst of pickling activity, but salad gardeners like to see weeks of production.

Parthenocarpic cucumbers are also around. These produce fruit but need no pollination and set no seeds. They are the latest rage in the cucumber world. These seedless cukes are a European greenhouse product, and they are found increasingly on American produce counters at around one dollar per fruit!

An outdoor type that combines features of the gynoecious and parthenocarpic plants gives good results if they are planted in an isolated area where bees are unlikely to pollinate them with ordinary cuke pollens.

Cucumber yields in home gardens can be increased by growing the plants as upright vines on stakes or wires, rather than letting them sprawl over the ground.

Nine cucumber cultivars, including special types from Australia, are offered by The Urban Farmer, and two samplers of mixed cultivars are available. Attractive to the curious is the Australian CRYSTAL SALAD cucumber, a short, lemon-shaped fruit with white skin, and SUYO LONG, native to northern China, which grows up to 15 inches long. J. L. Hudson carries WEST INDIAN GHERKIN and BOSTON PICKLING cucumber, both famous old pickling types. (The unusual West Indian Gherkin is *Cucumis anguria*, much prized in the past for sweet pickles.) Vermont Bean Seed offers several pickler types, all open-pollinated, along with half a dozen slicers and some of the new bush cucumbers for gardeners with little space. (Cucumber fences and trellises allow one to grow standards in less space than the dwarf bush types take up.) Nichols Garden Nursery has 13 slicer or salad cucumbers, including the new SWEET SUCCESS, a gynoecious-parthenocarpic hybrid that gives sweet and seedless cucumbers and may be grown outdoors. They also have two gynoecious forcing hybrids, GOURMET #2 and FEMBABY. Gourmet and Fembaby are intended for greenhouse growing. Nichols also sells six pickling types of cucumber, including the famous French CORNICHON DE BOURBONNE for making the hard, sour little pickles so good with cold roasts. Here the cucumber fancier will also find the YARD-LONG ARMENIAN that makes excellent Greek cucumber salads with yogurt and garlic.

Thompson and Morgan are very strong in the gynoecious greenhouse cukes, and offer MILDANA, Fembaby, KOSURA, TOPSY, and UNIFLORA. Seed costs as much as $3.95 for five seeds, but ten plants should produce a minimum of 50 pounds of fruit over the long season—that's fifty bucks' worth at your friendly neighborhood supermarket.

It is in the salad bowl that the cucumber becomes the prince of vegetables. Sliced and drained cucumbers are good in most green salads. Only young, firm cucumbers whose seeds have not set, or gynoecious cucumbers are fit for the salad bowl. Once the seeds of monoecious cucumbers start to harden, the cucumber takes on a fermented flavor and the seeds are unpleasant in the salad. Nearly every cuisine has a cucumber salad among its gifts to the table. Here are a few of thousands.

Classic Cucumber Salad

Wash freshly picked young cucumbers and chill them several hours. Score the skins with longitudinal grooves with the tine of a fork, and then slice them very thin. (Part or all of the skins may be peeled away if you prefer.) Let the slices drain on cheesecloth for 30 minutes. Put them in a glass bowl and dress with vinaigrette seasoned with chervil and chopped shallots.

Greek Cucumber Salad

Years ago a friend of mine, Michael Minsky, went to Greece for his first trip abroad. He came back with wonderful memories and a recipe for a delicious cucumber salad. The simple recipe passed from hand to hand among his friends and acquaintances, and now, hundreds of people in Vermont make this fine dish.

    5 or 6 garden-fresh cucumbers
        1 quart good-quality yogurt
        1 clove garlic
           pepper to taste
           lettuce leaves
           Greek olives

Peel and coarsely grate the young cucumbers. Place them in a cheesecloth bag and let them drain. In another cheesecloth bag, drain the yogurt. Gently squeeze the excess liquid from both cucumbers and yogurt at the end of an hour or two. Mix them together in a glass bowl. Add the garlic pressed through a crusher. Season with pepper.

Chill until cold and serve on chilled beds of lettuce with Greek olives.

6 servings

VARIATIONS: There are hundreds of variations of this basic cucumber-yogurt salad. One is Turkish Cucumber Salad.

Turkish Cucumber Salad

        2 young cucumbers
        2 tablespoons golden raisins
        1 cup yogurt
        2 tablespoons lemon juice
        2 tablespoons chopped almonds
        2 tablespoons chopped fresh mint
        1 clove garlic, crushed
        1 teaspoon chopped chives
       ¼ teaspoon Tamari

Seed, grate, and drain the cucumbers. Boil the raisins in water until plump and drain.

Combine all of the ingredients listed above.

Chill the salad and serve with finely chopped lettuce heaped on individual salad plates.

5 to 6 servings

Chinese Cucumber Salad

      3 to 4 cucumbers
            2 tablespoons lemon juice or rice wine vinegar
            1 clove garlic, crushed
            1 teaspoon chopped Chinese chives or other small onions
            1 tablespoon soy sauce
          ½ teaspoon chopped fresh ginger stem
               sesame seed oil

Choose fine young cucumbers from the garden. Wash them, score with fork tines, or cut longitudinal shallow grooves in the skin with a paring knife. Slice the cucumbers very thin, and put them in a glass or ceramic bowl.

Combine the lemon juice or vinegar, garlic, chives or onions, soy sauce, and ginger.

Let this mixture stand several hours in the refrigerator. Drain the cucumbers just before serving and mix in a few drops of sesame seed oil until the slices are lightly oiled. Pour the dressing over the cucumbers and serve.

6 to 8 servings

Russian Cucumber and Radish Salad

The cucumber is practically the Russian national vegetable, and while they are consumed out of hand in that country, what the Russians can do with a few cucumbers and some sour cream is legendary.

            4 young cucumbers, sliced
    4 or 5 red or pink radishes, sliced very thin
        1½ cups sour cream
            1 tablespoon wine or cider vinegar
            1 teaspoon honey
            1 tablespoon minced dill
               freshly ground pepper

Chill the cucumber slices and radishes separately in the refrigerator for an hour. Drain both if necessary.

Mix together in a glass bowl the sour cream, vinegar, honey, dill, and pepper. Stir the cucumber and radish slices into the dressing until well mixed. Serve very cold.

8 servings

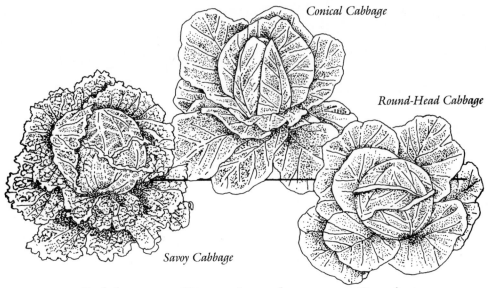

Conical Cabbage

Round-Head Cabbage

Savoy Cabbage

Cabbages (*Brassica oleracea,* Capitata Group)

The brassicas include more than 40 species of annuals and biennials of Old World origin. Here are the cabbages, broccoli, kale, coleworts, cauliflower, kohlrabi, rape, bok choy, Chinese cabbage, turnips, mustards, and many other brassica relatives that sometimes overlap each other in confusion. Batty Langley avoided the issue of what was cabbage and what was colewort by writing, "To make an Attempt of informing Mankind what a Cabbage, Savoy or Colly-flower is, would be both a ridiculous and simple Thing, seeing that every Person living are perfectly acquainted therewith; and therefore I will, instead thereof, mention such Kinds as are worth our Notice." I feel the same way.

Brassica oleracea counts many cultivars in sizes, shapes, seasons, and colors. Savoy cabbages are beautiful plants with blistered, puckery leaves, much admired by the ceramic artists who design soup tureens. Cabbages are generally divided into seasonal types—early, midseason, and winter or storage cabbages.

Wild cabbage of good flavor still grows along the chalk cliffs of England and France. This weedy plant is the ancient ancestor of our thick-headed domestic types. The Egyptians, who had unusual relationships with vegetables, are said to have worshipped cabbage, and the Greeks worked it into their mythology as the solidified product of the pearls of sweat that stood on Jupiter's brow as he tried to puzzle out two contradictory oracles. The Romans were under the impression that cabbage leaves eaten before a banquet could stave off drunkenness, and John Gerard, writing centuries later, explained this by citing such animosity between grapevines and cabbages, that the vines would die if cabbage were planted nearby—hence the power of cabbage over wine.

Gerard names 16 kinds of cabbage including savoy and red cabbages and lists many medicinal uses for cabbage from clearing the complexion to curing deafness. John Winthrop, Jr. brought "1 oz Cabedg seed" along in his seed chest when he came to the Bay Colony, and almost a hundred years earlier Jacques Cartier had planted cabbages in Canada on his third voyage to that cold northern land.

Batty Langley named the leading cabbages of his day. "The best Kinds of Cabbages are those which, tho' firm, close, and very large, yet are very light, as the true Sugar-loaf, the early white *Batterfea*, and the *French* cabbage; and of Savoys the same. But of all the several Kinds, the curdled Savoy, yellow in the middle, environed with deep green curdled Leaves, is, of all others, the most beautiful, sweetest, and despises the Severity of our Winters Frosts, which the other Kinds will not."

The cabbages are well suited to the north, for they tolerate light frosts and thrive in such cold damp climates as Holland,

---

Hally on a Cabbage Stalk

An old English rhyme was recited by girls on Halloween. One at a time, the girls would close their eyes and grope among the stalks of piled-up harvested cabbages and chant:

Hally on a cabbage stalk, and hally on a bean.
Hally on a cabbage stalk, tomorrow's Halloween.

The stalk her hand finally lighted upon, whether short or stout, crooked or thin, diseased or broken, was supposed to indicate the physical attributes of her future husband. Heaven knows to what ancient rites this custom was linked!

England, and the Scandinavian countries. Bernard M'Mahon mentions seven early cabbage types and six late winter keeping cabbages in his 1806 list. Late in the century Vilmorin-Andrieux named more than 50 kinds of cabbage cultivars in *The Vegetable Garden*.

Cabbages are the victims of many kinds of fungus, and they are alluring to insects, especially root maggots. Cabbage worms and aphids take their toll. Commercial preparations of *Bacillus thuringiensis* can be used to very good effect against cabbage worms and are harmless to humans. Club-root fungus is avoided by long crop rotations that keep the brassica groups out of soil inhabited by relatives from four to six years.

Gardeners and fruit growers who attend the New York State Fruit Testing Association's day for members every September may not realize that they are in the sauerkraut-cabbage capital of the United States. Incredible fields of cabbage stretch for miles around the little town of Phelps, and visitors can buy a station-wagon full of gigantic kraut cabbages for only a few dollars. I can never resist the mild, flat-topped "Dutch" cabbage bought right out of the fields for homemade sauerkraut.

Cabbages do not seem to excite the seed companies. They all appear to offer three to five of the same varieties: STONEHEAD, EARLY JERSEY WAKEFIELD, RED ROCK, and BALLHEAD. Ho hum. Nichols Garden Nursery has a fuller list than most, but Thompson and Morgan's cabbage section offers 17 cabbage cultivars, excluding the oriental types. Here one can choose from early, midseason or late cabbages in sizes and shapes to suit any grower's fancy.

*T*urnips *are included in Langley's list of good salad ingredients. He says, "The Seed Leaves when eaten in Salleting, the Roots when boil'd, and the tender Tops in the Spring for Soup."*

John Evelyn was not excited about the salad possibilities of cabbage, and puzzles to himself why the ancient Greeks and Romans thought so highly of the plant. Cabbage does not go well in the mixed green salad bowl because of its strong flavor, tougher leaf, and coarse texture. It is a mistake to introduce it there. It is better treated like a solitary jewel whose splendor is set off by lesser lights.

Red Cabbage Marinade

Unusual in this country, but very popular in Europe, is the marinade salad. One finds this everywhere in Germany and Switzerland, and it is worth making here. This pickled salad is traditionally used as a side-dressing for cold meats.

    1 head red cabbage
    1 crushed bay leaf
    1 clove garlic, crushed
       several peppercorns
       vinegar

Wash, trim, and core a red cabbage. Shred the cabbage or grate it coarsely. Put the shredded cabbage in a glazed earthenware bowl. Let this stand at room temperature for two days, stirring from time to time.

Drain the cabbage. Add to the bowl the bay leaf, garlic, and peppercorns. Cover all with a good-quality vinegar and allow the cabbage to marinate another day or two before draining and serving.

8 servings

Coleslaw

A very quick and easy cabbage salad is made with grated cabbage, grated carrot, a few tablespoons of chopped golden raisins, a pinch of crushed caraway seeds, a chopped apple of good flavor, and any mayonnaise dressing. This is kin to a hundred coleslaw recipes, and as everyone has a favorite coleslaw and every cookbook features half a dozen ways of making slaw, I'll not add to the throng.

Simple Cabbage Salad

1 head cabbage
French dressing
prepared mustard
tarragon to taste

Choose a young, tender-fleshed but firm cabbage from the garden. Wash it, trim off the tougher outer leaves and cut out the core. Cut or shred the cabbage into very fine strips as thin as string. Put these in a glass bowl and cover with ice water and soak for an hour.

Drain the cabbage and spin it dry in a salad greens spinner.

Serve cold and crisp with a French dressing to which 1 teaspoon of prepared mustard has been added. Tarragon (go easy on the fresh stuff) gives this simple salad a fine bouquet.

8 to 10 servings

VARIATIONS: Any vinaigrette or herb dressing or creamy dressing can be used in this salad, and a blue cheese dressing is surprisingly good.

August Cabbage Salad

This is a fine salad to make on a hot August morning. It is cold and delicious for accompanying an evening barbecue.

1 head of cabbage
1 cup sour cream
1 teaspoon prepared mustard
chopped dill to taste
2 tablespoons minced dill pickle
2 tablespoons minced shallot
2 tablespoons minced green pepper
ground pepper to taste
a few drops of lemon juice

Choose a small, firm head of new cabbage. Wash, trim, and shred the cabbage fine into a glass bowl.

Mix the remaining ingredients to make the dressing. Blend this mixture into the cabbage and chill in the refrigerator several hours before serving.

8 to 10 servings

Kohlrabi

Kohlrabi (*Brassica oleracea,* Gongylodes Group)

Kohlrabi, or "turnip cabbage," is appreciated by only a few knowing gardeners, but these elect know it as one of the most handsome and delicious of vegetables. The stem swells near the ground into a thick ball, ranging in size from a hen's egg to a sphere nearly as large as an iceberg lettuce. Most types are at their best when the tuberous stem is no larger than 3 inches in diameter.

Kohlrabi is a relatively new vegetable, apparently unknown to the ancients. It generally appears in two types, the green and the purple, but the French have several fancy-leaved decorative kinds as well.

Kohlrabi is grown as are turnips—sown *in situ* and thinned to about 10 inches apart in the bed or row. The plants can be sown every ten days from early spring into late summer for succession crops. Like radishes and turnips, fast growth in cool, damp weather produces the most tender kohlrabi. Because it is a brassica, it is troubled by the same pests and diseases that afflict cabbages and broccoli and other cole crops. It should be carefully rotated and kept out of soil used up to three seasons before for these related crops. Generally the brassica crops should follow peas, beans, lettuce, or onions.

Kohlrabi is not recognized by very many as a salad plant, Andre Simon mentions in *A Concise Encyclopedia of Gastronomy* a salad made of kohlrabi "shaved fine" and served with a mayonnaise dressing. I have discovered that this very mild and good vegetable also makes an excellent salad when shredded julienne and added to mixed green salads.

Celery *(Apium graveolens* var. *dulce)*

Celery is also a newcomer to the garden and the salad bowl. In the wild it is a marsh-loving plant that grows from Sweden to Algeria, in India, Terra del Fuego, New Zealand, and California. It was known in ancient days, but according to one of E. Lewis Sturtevant's sources, it was considered "a funereal or ill-omened plant." Early garden writers referred to it as "smallage," and cultivated types began to appear, not for salad gardens, but for the physic gardens. John Parkinson said it was "much planted in gardens and although his evil taste and savour doth cause it not to be accepted in meates as Parsley, yet it is not without many special good properties, both for outward and inward diseases."

It is not until Evelyn that we find smallage improved enough to reach the salad bowl. He wrote: "The tender leaves of the Blancht Stalk do well in our Sallet, as likewise the slices of the whiten'd Stems, which being crimp and short, first peeled and slit long wise, are eaten with Oyl, Vinegar, Salt and Pepper, and for its high and grateful Taste is ever placed in the middle of the Grand Sallet . . . the Grace of the whole Board."

By the time Batty Langley wrote, celery was so well known he could say, "There is no Herb adds so rich a Flavour to our Spring Sallets, as blanch'd Sellery. It is a Herb generously hot, and very easily propagated. To describe this Herb would be a needless work, seeing that its great Use has made it universally known to every one. . . ." He recommends mixing celery with other salad herbs, and repeats Evelyn's recipe of sliced celery served vinaigrette, but adds a very fancy culinary touch, which may be practiced today to decorate a salad.

He says, "I have seen some Gardiners, who have been very curious in the splitting of the blanched Leaves of Sellery with a Pin, which being afterwards thrown into clean cold Water curl themselves up, and make a very agreeable Figure, when well disposed of amongst the other Sorts of Sallet Herbs."

Deep, rich, mellow garden soil that can hold moisture without being really wet is suitable for growing celery. For it to be tender, it needs a quick growing start and a rapid move toward maturity; slow-growing celery is tough celery. In home gardens, vitamin-conscious gardeners rarely bother to blanch celery any more, but have adapted their tastes to the stronger, richer flavors of an all-green celery and learned to love it. The home gardener who practices intercropping and has a damp cool soil, can grow very fine celery, far richer than anything in the supermarket.

GOLDEN SELF BLANCHING is the ubiquitous cultivar offered by nearly every seed company. This is an early dwarf type (115 days to maturity) that does not have many of the notorious celery strings. It is a rich yellow green color, a variation of the nineteenth century DWARF SOLID WHITE, and Golden was originally developed by a market gardener outside Paris. Redwood City Seed offers the TALL GOLDEN SELF-BLANCHING, a disease-resistant and taller plant than the dwarf Golden. SOLID WHITE and SOLID RED celeries can be found, too, the latter an English cultivar with a purple tinge to the stalks. This is a hardier kind than the Golden. J. L. Hudson, which offers Solid Red, also has the old cultivar GIANT PASCAL, a green type not meant to be blanched.

Andre Simon advises cutting celery very fine into matchsticks and serving it with a mustard-flavored dressing. The chilled matchsticks are equally good with a vinaigrette dressing. The stalks may be cut in larger pieces, poached until tender in broth or water, then drained or chilled, and served on beds of lettuce or watercress with any dressing. Most of us, however, like our celery crunchy and raw.

Sources for Seeds

Alston Seed Growers
P.O. Box 266
Littleton, NC 27850

Bountiful Gardens
John Jeavons
5798 Ridgewood Rd.
Willits, CA 95490

W. Atlee Burpee Co.
Warminster, PA 18974

Butterbrooke Farm Seed Corp.
78 Barry Rd.
Oxford, CT 06483

Comstock, Ferre & Co.
263 Main St.
Wethersfield, CT 06109

The Cook's Garden
Londonderry, VT 05148

Epicure Seeds Ltd.
P.O. Box 450
Brewster, NY 10509

Ferry-Morse Seed Co. (wholesaler)
111 Ferry-Morse Way
Mountain View, CA 94040

Garden City Seeds
Box 297
Victor, MT 59875

Gleckler Seedsmen
Metamora, OH 43450

Greenleaf Seeds
P.O. Box 89
Conway, MA 01341

Gurney Seed & Nursery Co.
Yankton, SD 57079

Harris Seeds
Joseph Harris Co., Inc.
Moreton Farm
3670 Buffalo Rd.
Rochester, NY 14624

Hastings
Seedsman to the South
434 Marietta St., N.W.
P.O. Box 4274
Atlanta, GA 30302

Herb Gathering, Inc.
Gourmet Seeds
5742 Kenwood
Kansas City, MO 64110

Herbst Brothers Seedsmen, Inc.
1000 N. Main St.
Brewster, NY 10509

J. L. Hudson, Seedsman[1]
P.O. Box 1058
Redwood City, CA 94064

Johnny's Selected Seeds
Albion, ME 04910

D. Landreth Seed Co.[1]
2700 Wilmarco Ave.
Baltimore, MD 21223

Le Jardin du Gourmet
West Danville, VT 05873

Le Marche[1]
Seeds International
P.O. Box 566
Dixon, CA 95620

Nichols Garden Nursery
1190 N. Pacific Highway
Albany, OR 97321

George W. Park Seed Co., Inc.
P.O. Box 31
Greenwood, SC 29646

Plants of the Southwest
1570 Pacheco St.
Santa Fe, NM 87501

Redwood City Seed Co.[1]
P.O. Box 361
Redwood City, CA 94064

Seed Savers Exchange[2]
203 Rural Ave.
Decorah, IA 52101

Seeds Blum
Idaho City Stage
Boise, ID 83706

Southern Exposure Seed Exchange
Rt. 1, Box 150
Esmont, VA 22937

Stokes Seeds Inc.
737 Main St.
Box 548
Buffalo, NY 14240

Suffolk Herbs
Sawyers Farm
Little Cornard
Sudbury, Suffolk
England CO1-00PF

Thompson & Morgan, Inc.
P.O. Box 100
Farmingdale, NJ 07727

Otis Twilley Seed Co., Inc.
P.O. Box 65
Trevose, PA 19047

The Urban Farmer Inc.
Box 22198
Beachwood, OH 44122

Vermont Bean Seed Co.
Garden Lane
Bomoseen, VT 05732

Vesey's Seeds, Ltd.
York, Prince Edward Island
Canada C0A 1P0

William Dam Seeds Limited
P.O. Box 8400
Dundas, Ontario
Canada L9H 6M1

---

[1]Inquire regarding the minimal cost for a catalog.

[2]This organization functions as a seed exchange, and no seeds are for sale. It publishes *Vegetable Variety Inventory* that lists commercial sources for heirloom cultivars.

Selected Bibiliography

Baker, Margaret. *Discovering the Folklore of Plants*. Aylesburg, England: Shire Publications, 1969, 1980.

Chan, Peter, with Gill, Spencer. *Better Vegetable Gardens the Chinese Way*. Portland, Oreg.: Graphic Arts Center Publishing Co., 1977.

Coats, Alice M. *Flowers and Their Histories*. New York: McGraw-Hill, 1968, 1971.

Creasy, Rosalind. *The Complete Book of Edible Landscaping*. San Francisco: Sierra Club Books, 1982.

Culpeper, Nicholas. *The Complete Herbal*. Cedar Knolls, N.J.: Wehman Brothers, 1960.

Dahlen, Martha, and Phillips, Karen. *A Popular Guide to Chinese Vegetables*. New York: Crown Publishers, 1983.

Editors of *Organic Gardening* magazine. *Gourmet Gardening*. Emmaus, Pa.: Rodale Press, 1978.

Evelyn, John. *Acetaria: A Discourse of Sallets*. Facsimile ed. published by Prospect England. Charlottesville, Va.: University Press of Virginia, 1983.

Foster, Gertrude B., and Louden, Rosemary F. *Park's Success with Herbs*. Greenwood, S.C.: George W. Park Seed Co., 1980.

Gerard, John. *The Herbal or General History of Plants*. Reprint of 1633 ed. New York: Dover, 1975.

Gibbons, Euell. *Stalking the Wild Asparagus*. New York: David McKay Co., 1962.

Grigson, Geoffrey. *An Englishman's Flora*. London: Hart-Davis, 1955.

Harrington, Geri. *Grow Your Own Chinese Vegetables*. New York: Collier Books, 1978.

Hedrick, U. P., ed. *Sturtevant's Notes on Edible Plants*. Report of New York Agricultural Experiment Station. Albany, N.Y.: New York Agricultural Experiment Station, 1919.

Henisch, Bridget Ann. *Fast and Feast: Food in Medieval Society*. University Park, Pa.: Pennsylvania State University Press, 1977.

Jabs, Carolyn. *The Heirloom Gardener*. San Francisco: Sierra Club Books, 1984.

James, Theodore, Jr. *The Gourmet Gardens*. New York: E. P. Dutton, 1983.

Langley, Batty. *New Principles of Gardening*. Edited by John D. Hunt. English Landscape Garden Series. New York: Garland Publishing, 1982.

Larkcom, Joy. *The Salad Garden*. New York: Viking Press, 1984.

Leighton, Ann. *Early American Gardens "For Meate or Medicine."* Boston: Houghton Mifflin Co., 1970.

Norman, Barbara. *Tales of the Table*. Englewood Cliffs, N.J.: Prentice-Hall, 1972.

Parkinson, John. *Paradisi in Sole, Paradisus Terrestris, or a Garden of All Sorts of Pleasant Flowers Which Our English Ayre Will Permit*. Reprint of 1629 ed. Norwood, N.J.: Walter J. Johnson, 1975.

Peterson, Lee. *A Field Guide to Edible Wild Plants*. Boston: Houghton Mifflin Co., 1978.

Powell, Thomas, and Powell, Betty. *The Avant Gardener*. Boston: Houghton Mifflin Co., 1975.

Root, Waverly. *Food*. New York: Simon and Schuster, 1980.

Shewell-Cooper, W. E. *Herbs, Salads and Tomatoes*. Rev. ed. London: John Gifford, 1972.

Simon, Andre, ed. *A Concise Encyclopedia of Gastronomy*. London: Wine and Food Society, 1941, 1948.

Truax, Carol. *The Art of Salad Making*. Garden City, N.Y.: Doubleday & Co., 1968.

United States Department of Agriculture. *Composition of Food*. Handbook no. 8. Washington, D.C.: USDA, 1963.

Vilmorin-Andrieux. *The Vegetable Garden*. Reprint of 1885 English ed. Berkeley, Calif.: Ten Speed Press, 1981.

Warner, Charles Dudley. *My Summer in a Garden*. Reprint of 1871 ed. New York: AMS Press, 1977.

Wolf, Ray, ed. *Solar Growing Frame*. Emmaus, Pa: Rodale Press, 1980.

Index

Page numbers in **boldface** indicate tables, boxes, and marginalia; page numbers in *italics* indicate illustrations.

203